CROP CIRCLES

HISTORY, RESEARCH AND THEORIES

Blowingstone Hill 6th August 2007 (Photo: Axel Kayser)

EVA-MARIE BREKKESTØ

CROP CIRCLES

HISTORY, RESEARCH AND THEORIES

Credits and Acknowledgements

This edition published in English in 2011 by Wessex Books
10 Thistlebarrow Road, Salisbury, Wiltshire, SP13RU
Tel: 01722 349695
Web: www.wessexbooks.co.uk
Email: info@wessexbooks.co.uk
UK Artwork www.kf-d.com

ISBN 978-1-903035-38-2

First published in Norwegian by Vega Forlag AS in Oslo 2010
Translated by Graham Timmins at The Right Word
Designed by Cecilie Mohr

Photographs

Front Cover by Olivier Morel
Back Cover Top: Axel Kayser,
Middle: Clas Svahn, Bottom: Axel Kayser

Printed in India

Winterbourne Bassett 31st July 2009 (Photo: Eva-Marie Brekkestø)

INDEX:

FOREWORD By Andy Thomas

It is now twenty years since I first set foot in an area of flattened plants, freshly swirled into an otherwise featureless field. The effect that moment had on me was profound and put my life on a very different path, as I embarked on a long, searching journey through my own belief systems. Where had this shape come from? What did it mean? What new paradigm was I prepared to accept in an effort to explain it?

Twenty years on, and the shocking truth is that those same questions about the crop circle mystery remain, and still no definitive answer has arrived. I have been involved in extensive research, organised events, lectured widely and written several books on this mercurial phenomenon and all manner of other seemingly paranormal mysteries and subsequent cover-ups - yet the origin and purpose of what started this journey continues to elude. Many other seekers, like the seasoned author of this book, have taken the same ride, and reached the same unavoidable conclusion that, when it comes to crop circles, the only certainty is the guarantee of uncertainty.

Calibrations, however, can be made, and important data can be sifted and filtered. From this process, a certain pattern, the faint notion of an ethos, does begin to emerge, and repeatable observations make themselves known. The idea that something is reaching out to us, either from afar, from the natural world or from deep within the collective mind, stimulating the development of consciousness by the very presence of uncertainty, is hard to entirely throw off. Whatever the reality, what does become clear from important factual assessments of the crop circles such as this book, is that in them we have a phenomenon far more rooted in history than most people are aware of, and one that deserves much greater contemplation than it has received from a dismissive mainstream media more interested in the scandals of human deception than in the impressive evidence which shows that there must be more to the story than simply hoaxers' planks and ropes.

Everything from science to metaphysics, from mathematics to ufology, has had to be employed in the investigation of this remarkable and tenacious enigma. Eva-Marie

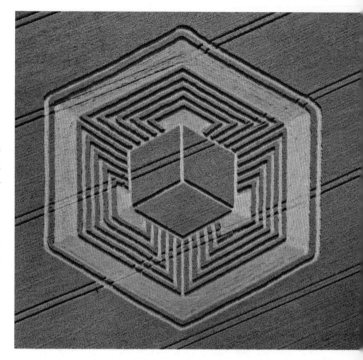

Above: Crop formation near Fosbury, Wiltshire, July 2010
(Photo: Eva-Marie Brekkestø)

Brekkestø, writing from her long experience in both the Norwegian and English crop fields, encapsulates well the data gathered from many of these approaches in her informed and balanced assessment of this beautiful, if frustratingly indefinable phenomenon. Commendably, the book deals with the facts and realities of what is happening in the fields without loading the dice with opinion and prejudice.

INTRODUCTION

Every summer, new crop circles bring thousands of people from all corners of the world to Wiltshire in southern England. Are they all just naive people surfing on the New Age wave, or have they discovered a phenomenon which is really worth looking into more closely? What exactly do we know about crop circles?

My aim with this book is to show that these are simply that, myths, and instead to present you with some facts.

The first time I saw pictures of crop circle, it was in a magazine in the mid-1990s. The article included large colour photos of English crop circles, and there was one picture which especially moved me: the triangular formation at Barbury Castle from 1991. I threw myself into exploring the phenomenon with great energy and excitement, eager to get some quick answers to all the questions that were bubbling up in me. I soon realized there were no quick answers. But after many years of studying the phenomenon, I decided it was time to share what I have learned.

With this book, my intention is to give a broad overview of the crop circle phenomenon. In it I share some of my own experiences and thoughts, but to a large extent it is a summary of previous research into the phenomenon as it has been presented in books, in films and on the internet. I must thank all of the researchers whose work I have drawn on, and also all my crop circle 'companions' in England, both those who live in the area and those who, like me, travel there every season to study the crop circles. Sometimes I even feel that the most important thing with my trips to Wiltshire is not the crop circles themselves but the meetings with all my much loved friends there! Without their sharing their experiences with me, I could not have written this book.

The writer G.K.Chesterton wrote in "On tremendous Trifles" (1909):
"The world will never starve for want of wonders, but only for want of wonder."
This book is dedicated to one of the most enchanting wonders of the world.

Jar, Bærum, Norway, April 2011 *Eva-Marie Brekkestø*

The famous triangular formation at Barbury Castle, July 1991.
(Photo: Richard Wintle)

CHAPTER 1

WHAT ARE CROP CIRCLES, AND WHERE DO THEY APPEAR?

In this chapter we'll look at what crop circles actually are, where and when they appear, and what possible explanations there might be for their prevalence in parts of southern England. Many people wonder whether formations which from time to time are discovered in soil, sand, ice and snow might also be connected with the crop circle phenomenon. At the end of the chapter we'll look more closely at some of these possibly related phenomena.

HOW DO WE DEFINE A CROP CIRCLE?

The term "crop circle" has become well established since the 1980s, when the first formations to be publicized were indeed simple circles in cornfields. However, it is slightly misleading, as the phenomenon appears as a great variety of complex shapes and patterns, by no means all of which even include a circle in the design. Nor is it

Facing page: Martinsell Hill 19th July 2009
(Photo Eva-Marie Brekkestø)

limited to agricultural crops: although the majority of formations do still appear in wheat and barley, rapeseed and maize have regularly been targeted, and the phenomenon has affected all sorts of plants, both cultivated and wild, including rice, field beans, carrots, flax, borage, heather, reeds, fodder grass, prairie grass, wild-flower meadows and fields of cultivated flowers. So, although 'crop circle' is still a useful term, I will also use other phrases such as "crop formations" or just "formations".

How then can we define a crop circle? Perhaps the nearest we can come is this: Living plants whose stems have been carefully bent or flattened in a precisely defined pattern. The bent or laid plants are usually undamaged, and continue to grow and mature if not damaged by other agencies.

WHERE AND WHEN DO CROP CIRCLES APPEAR?

The global picture is that crop circles appear in both cultivated and wild plants all year round. As long as there are plants growing, crop circles may occur.

In the northern hemisphere, the season for crop circles may last from April to October. The first formations of the spring in England, central Europe and North America are usually reported from the middle of April to the middle of May and are in oilseed rape fields. From the end of May, formations start appearing in young barley, and from the middle of June, wheat fields start to take over as the most typical setting. Winter barley (sown the previous autumn) is generally harvested towards the end of July, while the last fields of spring wheat (sown from February onwards) are often cut around the end of August, marking the end of the 'corn circle' season as such. In recent years however, crop circles have also appeared in maize fields in both Europe and North America, any time from late August to October. During the northern hemisphere's winter months, occasional formations have also been seen in grass and heather.

Crop circles also appear regularly in the southern hemisphere, although in much smaller numbers than in the northern hemisphere. During our winter months, crop circles have been reported from countries such as Brazil, Australia, New Zealand, South Africa and most recently Indonesia. The types of locations have ranged from different types of cornfields and grasslands to rice paddies and reed beds.

At the time of writing, there are records of over 7000 crop circles world-wide, and that's only those which have been reported to researchers, registered or mentioned in the media. How many others appear but are never reported, we cannot say. In recent years several hundred formations have been recorded annually. In Europe, records come from about 20 different countries, from Italy and Spain in the south to Norway and Sweden in the north, from Russia in the east to France and Britain in the west.

Before the 1980s it seems that crop formations were mostly simple patterns based on circles of flattened crop, although there are also a few reports of more complex patterns. Nevertheless there was a clear development towards the end of the millennium, whereby crop circle patterns gradually became both larger and more complex. This trend was more obvious in England than in other parts of the world. Around half of all crop circles which appear world-wide do so in England, and the great majority of these are found in a relatively small area of southern England, the ancient kingdom of Wessex.

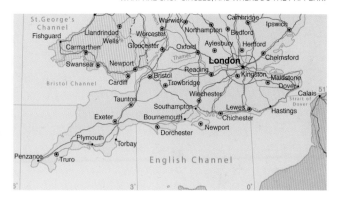

Map of southern England

THE LEGENDARY LANDSCAPE OF SOUTHERN ENGLAND

Around 90% of English crop circles appear regularly in the counties of Wiltshire, Hampshire, Berkshire and Oxfordshire. Some formations are also reported from Sussex, Kent, Gloucestershire, Warwickshire and further afield, according to the year. The core area though is without doubt the county of Wiltshire, and specifically the northern half of the county. The heartlands of the crop circle phenomenon are in fact the chalk downlands south of Swindon, in an area which includes the market towns of Marlborough and Devizes and the village of Avebury. Why do so many crop circles appear in just this area?

The counties of southern England, with the county of Wiltshire in the middle.

SOUTHERN ENGLAND IN PREHISTORIC TIMES

It seems that Wiltshire was already a very special place in Neolithic times. As far back as 3,500 years BC, the local inhabitants had erected numerous huge monuments on a scale such as is scarcely found anywhere else in Europe. The earliest constructions were the impressive 'long barrows', up to 100m long passage graves, built of huge stones and covered with earth. These were not graves in the modern sense, but ceremonial places where human bones were temporarily preserved before final burial

Crop Circle close to Wayland's Smithy long barrow, Oxfordshire August 2005 (photo: Steve Alexander)

elsewhere. The best known and best preserved of these are at West Kennet and Wayland's Smithy, both of which are places where spectacular crop circles appear with great regularity.

The largest stone circle in the world, at Avebury, was begun in about 2,900 BC, at the same time as Silbury Hill, the biggest prehistoric mound in Europe, whose purpose and significance can still only be guessed at. Every single year, several new crop circles appear in fields right next to or overlooking these monuments. Stonehenge, where construction started in about 2,600 BC, has also been the venue for a number of crop circles over the years, even though it is to the south of the core area for crop circle activity. Iron Age hill forts dating from 700 BC onwards, visible today only as a ring or series of banks and ditches, abound in the area, and these are also popular locations for crop circles to appear. The best known of these feature spectacular crop circles every season and include Oliver's Castle, Cherhill, Barbury Castle, Liddington Castle and Uffington Castle.

Another type of Iron Age monument is the burial mound or tumulus, nowadays most likely overgrown with grass or trees and often referred to as a knoll. These were built by Celtic [1] tribes who were colonizing England in the second half of the first millennium BC. Numerous corn circles have appeared next to and been named after these knolls over the years. Another feature of the Wiltshire downs is the Ridgeway, an ancient track way which leads from Salisbury plain to the Chilterns and ultimately to the East Anglian coast. Parts of it may have been used to transport sarsen stones from Marlborough Downs to Stonehenge. Today a part of the trackway is incorporated into the Ridgeway National Trail, which is a popular long distance footpath and bridleway. Parts of the Ridgeway are known to be at least five thousand years old; it passes right through the heart of crop circle country.

Even a brief glance at some of outstanding features of the Wiltshire landscape must include a mention of the famous 'white horses', hill figures which have been created in several parts of England, but most notably in the Wiltshire down lands, by cutting away the turf to expose the chalk bedrock. There are about 20 in England,

Facing page: Crop formation with Avebury henge in the background, August 2005 (photo: Steve Alexander)

---

1 It's a widespread misconception that the Celts and their Druid priests had anything to do with the building of Stonehenge or Avebury. The Celtic tribes began to spread from northern Spain and France to the British Isles around 500 B.C., at least 2,000 years after those monuments were constructed.

Top: Formation in oilseed rape at Oliver's Castle, Wiltshire, April 2007.
The ramparts of Oliver's Castle are seen on the left hand side
(Photo: John Montgomery)
Bottom: Wayland's Smithy passage grave in Oxfordshire
(Photo: Eva-Marie Brekkestø)

Facing page: Crop circle formation under the White Horse at Milk Hill,
Alton Barnes, 2009
(Photo: Eva-Marie Brekkestø)

but only the one at Uffington in Oxfordshire is known to be of prehistoric origin, while most of the 8 surviving in Wiltshire are Victorian. Nevertheless many of them seem to attract crop circles, and the white horses at Westbury, Hackpen and Alton Barnes in particular very often find themselves gazing down upon new crop formations in the fields below.

WHY SOUTHERN ENGLAND?

Crop circle enthusiasts visiting England are fascinated by the striking way the formations are often placed in relation to ancient monuments. They regularly appear in the same fields as Neolithic burial mounds, hill forts and stone circles, and those with geometric designs are sometimes aligned to point directly towards the ancient sites. The impressive prehistoric remains and today's beautiful crop formations seem to complement each other visually and in a way to reinforce each others' significance. Is there a connection between the two, or is it just coincidence?

One theory which has been proposed is that the crop circles actually came first. If the people who lived here 5 to 6 thousand years ago found circles appearing in the grass or in their cultivated land, and noticed that they re-occurred year after year in roughly the same locations, then these sites might have come to be regarded as sacred. Once they became cult sites, over time first wooden and then stone circles or mounds might have been built.

Throughout unrecorded and recorded history, crop circles continued to appear near these sacred sites, so the theory goes, and so it has continued down to the present day, when they once again are being taken notice of.

Alternatively, have the crop circles been deliberately placed so as to draw our attention to the ancient monuments? After England was converted to Christianity, the stone circles, burial mounds and other pagan sacred sites were abandoned, and many were deliberately damaged or destroyed. Only in the 19th century did serious historical interest in them arise again, when archaeologists began to investigate and restore them. In the 1970s, something quite new happened, however. As the New Age dawned over England, a section of the general public began to be interested in the ancient monuments again and to explore their spiritual relevance. With the revival of Paganism and indeed Druidism, places like Stonehenge and Avebury began to regain something of their original function as temples or cult sites.

When crop circles began to attract interest in the 1980s, their placement close to

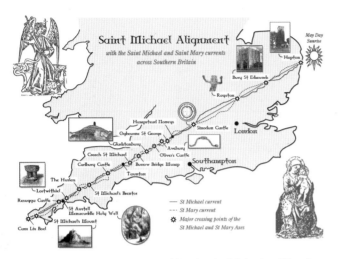

Map showing Michael and Mary lines

Caduceus or Thoth's holy staff

Facing page: Crop circle at Roundway Hill near Devizes, with a burial mound in the background, July 2010 (Photo: Eva-Marie Brekkestø)

the ancient monuments was immediately observed and the idea arose that the circles appeared where they did in order to lead our attention to the sacred sites. Today the crop circles' positioning still invites us to rediscover the ancient holy places and their spiritual significance.

A third way of linking these two features of the Wessex landscape might be to say there is a common reason for the placement of both crop circles and ancient monuments. In the next section we will look at the concept of ley lines, or earth energy lines as they are often called nowadays. Later in the book we will explore geological theories for the occurrence of crop circles in southern England (chapter 6).

ENERGY LINES

As early as the late 19th century, archaeologists and naturalists in England had discussed the placement of ancient monuments and churches in the landscape in such a way as to form straight lines. In 1921 Alfred Watkins published *The Old Straight Track*, in which he suggested that these placements were not accidental, and coined the term 'ley lines' to denote the pathways he found between hilltop forts and other monuments, which he interpreted as trading routes. Dowsers investigating alignments of ancient monuments in the 1930s, however, linked their locations to underground streams or to magnetic currents. Gradually the emphasis shifted with the decades so that 'ley line' came to mean an energetic pathway of some sort, even though writers such as Guy Underwood, who popularized archaeological dowsing in the 1960s, continued to develop a terminology based on water dowsing, including features such as 'water lines', 'aquastats' and 'blind springs'. With an upsurge in interest in dowsing in the 1980s, whether using dowsing rods or pendulums, the term 'energy line' came into use and many new kinds of such energy lines were classified. Parallels have also been drawn between earth energy lines, found in a network all over the planet, and energy lines or meridians in the human body such as are described in Chinese medicine.

Some earth energy lines seem to extend over a long distance, and the most significant one in southern England, first proposed by John Michell, has been called the Michael line as it passes through a number of churches and villages named after St. Michael. It leads from Land's End in Cornwall all the way across southern England, passing north of London to come out on the North Sea coast at Hopton in Norfolk, and joining together ancient monuments such as St. Michael's Mount, Glastonbury Tor, Oliver's

Facing page: Michael line (red) and Mary line (green) where they pass through the area around Avebury, according to Broadhurst and Miller. The blue line indicates the central axis (the Great Dragon ley) which the two lines entwine around (Illustration: Hamish Miller)

Castle, Avebury and Uffington Castle. Place names which are very familiar to crop circle enthusiasts!

Another line, called the Old Sarum Ley, was one of the first ley lines identified by Watkins. It comes in from the English Channel in the south, passing through Salisbury Cathedral, Old Sarum hill fort, Stonehenge, Marden Henge and the Avebury complex.

Hamish Miller and Paul Broadhurst, two British dowsers with long experience of dowsing the sacred sites of southern England, decided in the 1980s to undertake a gigantic project: to follow the Michael line from beginning to end. The project took up most of their free time over a number of years and is described in their book *The Sun and the Serpent*. Starting off in Cornwall, the dowsers soon found that the energy line they were tracking was not actually straight, but wavering. After two years, when Broadhurst and Miller had got as far as the Avebury area, they made an even more startling discovery which sent them back to square one: on the site of the former stone circle known as the Sanctuary, now destroyed, they dowsed another energy line crossing the 'Michael' line. Nothing unusual in itself, for the whole of southern England is criss-crossed by a network of minor energy lines, according to dowsers. This new line however seemed to be just as strong as the Michael line, but in contrast to the latter's 'masculine' energy, it had a different and to them clearly 'feminine' energy. They called this St. Mary's line and followed it a short way back through the countryside. Soon it became clear that the two lines were constantly crossing each other. Broadhurst and Miller decided to go right back to where they had started at Land's End and see if they could pick up the Mary line there as well.

Broadhurst and Miller found that the Michael and Mary lines are entwined around a common axis like a twisted braid. Neither of them are actually straight, but the axis that they follow is. The way the energy lines cross at significant points on the landscape, marked by ancient sacred sites, made the dowsers think of the Caduceus symbol. This ancient symbol depicts two serpents entwined around a staff, which is sprouting wings. Its history and mythology goes back at least as far as ancient Egypt, where it was known as the god Thoth's holy staff, although it later picked up many other meanings and today is associated in the west with the medical and pharmacological professions. A crop formation which appeared at Milk Hill near Alton Barnes in 2004 also reminded some crop circle enthusiasts of this very symbol.

When Broadhurst and Miller had followed the two lines back to Wiltshire, they

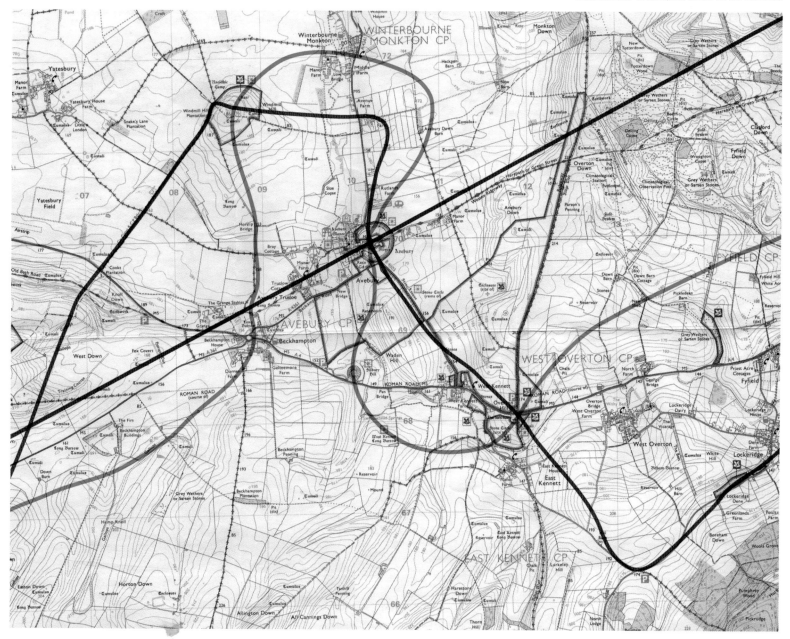

William Stukeley studied the Avebury complex in detail in the 18th century. This drawing shows how he envisaged the whole ceremonial landscape around Avebury

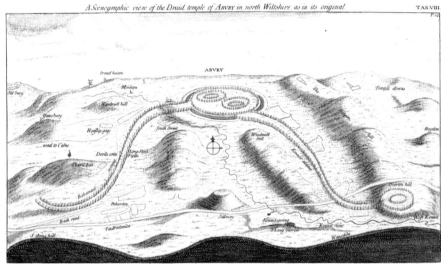

Facing page: The crop circle in the form of a figure of eight or infinity symbol, which appeared at Milk Hill on 08.08.08 (Photo: Axel Kayser)

discovered they crossed not only at the Sanctuary, but at Oliver's Castle, Windmill Hill and in the centres of each of the inner stone circles at Avebury henge. When I read the chapters on Wiltshire and Oxfordshire in *The Sun and the Serpent*, I noticed that nearly every place name mentioned is a significant crop circle location.

Broadhurst and Miller were not crop circle enthusiasts when they carried out their Michael and Mary line project, so they only mention the subject in passing in their book. However, when I spoke to Miller in 2008, he confirmed that he had subsequently been aware of the close connection between crop circles and the Michael and Mary lines. When I got to see Miller's detailed map of the lines' route through Wiltshire and Oxfordshire, I gazed at it in astonishment. The area between the lines covers many of the best known circle locations in these counties, with the possible exception of those in the Pewsey Vale area. And it just so happens that the Old Sarum line comes up from the south and crosses the Vale before it meets the Michael and Mary lines at Avebury. Miller also explained to me that the reason that some years more circles appear one side or the other of the line might be that the strength of the lines can vary from year to year in different places.

Avebury today

Facing page: Crop circle at Silbury Hill July 2009
(Photo: Eva-Marie Brekkestø)

AVEBURY

Avebury is the largest stone circle in the world and is now seen as the centre of a vast ceremonial landscape which formerly included two long stone avenues, the Silbury Hill pyramid and several other large circular henges now lost. What's more, it's at the geographic centre of crop circle activity in Wessex, and so is central to the crop circle story.

The construction of Avebury began in Neolithic times, around 3000 BC, and about 200 years before Stonehenge phase 1 was begun. At 11.5 hectares (28 acres), Avebury encloses 14 times the area of Stonehenge, and archaeologists have no doubt that 4,500 years ago it was an extremely important religious centre which drew people from far and wide. The better known Stonehenge was a minor monument in this context.

The enormous bank and ditch which surrounds Avebury is over 427m (1401ft) in diameter. Archaeological digs have shown that the ditch was originally about 9m deep, and the bank constructed from the excavated material (which is now up to 6m high) is likely also to have been about the same height, giving a total height from top to bottom of around 18m. Estimates of the amount of solid chalk excavated by our Neolithic ancestors range around an incredible 100,000 cubic metres. When first constructed, the steep-sided bank and ditch of exposed chalk would have stood out shining white, though now they are eroded and overgrown with grass.

Within this enclosure and in the course of the next three centuries, 160 megaliths were raised, with some of those now remaining weighing over 40 tonnes and one giant calculated at over 100 tonnes. 98 sarsen stones were somehow dragged from the Marlborough Downs to form the main circle within the henge, while two separate large circles were aligned inside. Remains of two of these can be seen today, with 27 and 29 stones or stone positions respectively, and both had internal features as well. Outside the henge are further components of the extraordinary ritual landscape around Avebury. The West Kennet stone avenue, consisting of paired standing stones placed 15m apart and like the main henge monuments surviving today in a much damaged but partially restored form, leads past Waden Hill 1.5km south east to the 'Sanctuary', site of a former double stone circle now destroyed. Only traces remains of a second stone avenue of similar length, known as the Beckhampton Avenue, which previously led south-west and may have finished at the monuments known as the Longstones.

The strange rings in the snow in Tatarstan, Russia in December 2007

As if all these massive engineering projects were not enough, at the same time construction also began on Silbury Hill, less than 2km away, which after several hundred years would become the largest man made mound in Europe, over 40m in height and containing an estimated 250,000 cubic metres of material. Archaeologists have found a seven-stepped pyramidal construction under the present layers of eroded soil, but have no idea what the purpose could have been for the building of this extraordinary monument. We do know that it was never a burial mound and was not designed for any defensive purpose, as the flattened top was created much later in Anglo-Saxon times. Incidentally, Silbury Hill was not the only artificial mound built in Neolithic times in the Avebury area, with another smaller mound, Marlborough Mount (also known as Merlin's Mount), preserved in the grounds of Marlborough College, and traces of a similar one at Marden, in the Vale of Pewsey.

Today, visitors to the Avebury Henge find that it is bisected by a busy main road and to a large extent occupied by a typical English village with about 20 houses, a couple of shops and a pub. The process of secularization started in the 1st century AD, when the Roman invaders set up camp inside the conveniently defendable henge, and as time went by, Avebury became a trading centre and permanent settlement. We cannot know to what extent the place remained a cult centre after the introduction of Christianity in the second century and its dominance from the seventh century, but the megaliths remained largely undamaged not only through the Roman era but for a thousand years afterwards. From the 14th century on, we know that standing stones were deliberately toppled and buried, presumably representative of the Church's policy of suppressing folk customs and beliefs surviving from pagan times, but real damage was not done until the 18th century, when local inhabitants started to break up the stones to use them as building material.

The whole Avebury complex was plundered relentlessly from the 1720s onwards, and the tide was not to be reversed until the 1930s when Alexander Keiller, heir to the Keiller marmalade business, got involved. Keiller was a self-taught archaeologist and a pioneer of aerial archaeology who in 1928 had published the first ever book on the subject, "Wessex from the Air". In the mid-1930s he excavated the West Kennet Avenue and re-erected all the fallen and buried stones he found, marking the vacant holes with concrete pillars. He started a three-year dig at Avebury in 1937 and continued buying out the local farmers and landowners in order to restore the ceremonial landscape to its former grandeur. Many houses were demolished and their inhabitants moved to the new settlement which Keiller had built nearby at Avebury Trusloe. Unfortunately his fortune ran out, and the Second World War intervened, before he could complete this mammoth undertaking, but it is only thanks to Keiller that we see anything resembling a henge at Avebury today. In the 1950s the estate passed to the National Trust. 15 megaliths from the eastern quadrant are known to remain buried on site, and many more nearby structures are still known only from crop marks and ground radar surveys. Local enthusiasts continue to petition for the main road to be diverted and the remaining buried stones to be replaced, but so far without success.

But what was Avebury all for? Recent research about the purpose of Avebury was presented in the book *Avebury: Sun, Moon and Earth* by Maria Wheatley and Busty Taylor. The authors see the two inner stone circles as astronomical calendars. A gigantic 6.5m high obelisk previously stood in the centre of the southern circle. This could have functioned as a kind of sundial, casting shadows onto the stones around the circumference.

The northern stone circle, meanwhile, is believed to have functioned as a lunar calendar. Most of the original stones in the ring are now lost, but at the centre of the circle there remain two large megaliths from a feature known as the Cove. Originally there were two tall, slender, 'masculine' stones (only one is standing today), and one broad, lozenge-shaped 'feminine' stone. The weight of the latter has been estimated at about 100 tonnes, which makes it the largest megalith in Great Britain. Wheatley and Taylor believe amongst other things that the Cove was aligned with the point on the horizon where the moon has its most northerly rising every 18.61 years.

Returning to the main circle, we know that the henge was built with four gaps through the bank and ditch, aligned with the cardinal points, just like it has today, where the roads pass through. However, Aubrey Burl discovered that at the some point in time, the southern opening was moved slightly. The original opening lay a few metres to the east of the present position, where there now stand two large beech trees on the bank. The interesting thing is that one of the 'portal stones' which guard the southern entrance has a kind of 'seat' on its south-facing side, which is known as 'The Devil's Chair'. From this position, according to Wheatley and Taylor's calculations, one would have been able to observe the sunrise at the mid-winter solstice through the gap in the bank (Taylor and Wheatley 2008).

Ice pictogram from Snåsa, Norway, 2003. Still picture from video film. (Photo: Victoria Flasnes)

Above: In January 2009 a thin layer of snow covered the ground at Oliver's Castle. But not where a crop circle had been the previous August! (Photo: Matthew Williams)

Facing page: Crop circle at Oliver's Castle, August 2008 (Photo: Russell Stannard)

Still, there has to be more to account for the size and scale of the whole henge, not to mention the associated stone avenues and Avebury's relationship to Silbury Hill, Windmill Hill, and Britain's largest long barrows (Neolithic burial mounds) at nearby West and East Kennet. The best conclusion we can probably come to at this stage is that the complex as a whole fulfilled a number of interlocking religious and ceremonial functions, which may have varied or changed in emphasis over the centuries.

RELATED PHENOMENA

Circles and patterns don't only appear in growing crops and other plants. Geometric patterns are also found in ice, snow, sand and earth. Some of them clearly have no connection to the crop circle phenomenon when one looks into them carefully. However, there are some exceptions, one of which we will look into in detail below[2].

Ice and snow patterns are much more common than patterns in earth and sand. Simple circles in ice or snow-covered ice are fairly easy to explain. 'Ice circles' are not actually circles drawn in the ice, but circular ice floes, formed when water currents in the back eddy of a river bend cause the water mass to rotate while it is freezing. They can be perfectly circular and can survive the melting of the surrounding ice. Ice circles like these appear every winter both in North America and Scandinavia. But in at least one case a circular ice floe has also appeared in a lake, in Maryland, USA, in 2001. This consisted of a circle with a rectangular addition, which rather rules out the rotating currents process and is harder to explain as a natural phenomenon.

An entirely different type of ice formation was discovered at Snåsa in Norway in 2003, one which seems more connected to the crop circle phenomenon. It was spotted by a group of school children in a field near their school.

During a break between lessons at, on the morning of 11th December, 12-year old classmates Gjermund and Sivert were out in the school yard. They were talking about

2 Pictures and reports about all the formations mentioned below can be found at www.cropcirclesnorway.com

Ghost circle at Oliver's Castle, July 2009 (Photo: Russell Stannard)

the film Signs, which they wanted to see, because they'd heard it was about exciting patterns in corn fields. While they stood there chatting, one of them happened to glance down at a field next to the school. Something which looked like a pattern of snow was clearly visible in the field. The children were quite frightened by this at first as it seemed rather creepy after they had just been talking about crop circles. They were sure that the pattern hadn't been there the day before. They went and told their classmate Victoria, but there was no chance to investigate closer as lessons were about to start again.

After the school day was over, the children went to take a closer look at the strange pattern in the field. Now they saw that it wasn't actually a pattern of snow, but was made of solid ice. The pattern they described looks somewhat like a target card for air rifle shooting, with two concentric circles divided into quadrants and a bulls eye in the centre. The outer ring was about 10m in diameter and the bulls eye about 75cm. One of the dividing lines extended for several metres outside the circles. The whole pattern was in the form of an ice relief 2-3cm thick laid onto the withered grass. The lines were regular and accurate, but a little snow which had blown around the formation made the patterns look a bit messy from a distance (see picture p. 27). The temperature was about two degrees below freezing. The three friends went back to Victoria's house to fetch a video camera. By the time they got back, the time was already 15:30 and it was getting dark. Victoria filmed the pattern from a distance first, but when she got down to the field and was going to film it close up, the camera stopped working. Later it turned out that the freshly charged camera battery was damaged beyond repair. It could not be recharged anymore and had to be replaced.

During the course of the evening, it began to snow again. Next day when the children came back to look again in the daylight, the ground was covered in snow and the pattern had disappeared. But they swept away the snow in places and confirmed that the ice relief was still intact underneath. All these details were confirmed in an interview with the present author, which took place on the day after the first discovery. The children's parents and other adults in the village also went to see the ice formation at Snåsa, and although it remained covered in snow for the rest of the winter, it was still there the following spring when the snow started to melt.

The most impressive snow formations have been reported from Russia. Near to Moscow in 1990 a large spiral formation was found, accompanied by mysterious light phenomena, while patterns of concentric rings up to 20m in diameter appeared in the Urals in 2004, in Tatarstan and Yekaterinburg in 2007, 'etched' like furrows into the snow (see picture p. 26). In December 2010 a pattern of rings in the snow was reported from Gloucestershire, England.

In December 2009, two large patterns in snow were reported from Hoeven in the Netherlands, site of many previous crop circles and other paranormal phenomena discovered by Robbert van den Broeke. The patterns consisted of series of contiguous rings and loops in the snow. When Dutch crop circle researcher Roy Boschman visited the formations, he found it strange that snow appeared to have been removed from the tracks and not piled up alongside, and he could not find any footprints in the snow either. (See the section 'Related Phenomena' at www.cropcirclesnorway.com for more details).

GHOST FORMATIONS

Even after the fields have been harvested and there is no trace of a crop formation, its effects can linger on. Frequently, when the next year's crop is growing strongly the following spring, the pattern becomes visible again as an area of darker green or stronger growth. The exact patterns can be clearly replicated in this way if conditions are right, giving rise to what are called 'ghost formations'. It seems that something about the crop circles gives a boost to the soil in the places where the corn has been laid flat. Dutch crop circle researchers Bert Janssen and Janet Ossebaard have suggested that changes in soil chemistry such as increased crystallization of clay particles could be responsible (Swirled News 2002). Such changes have been confirmed in many crop circles, a subject we'll return to in chapter 6. However many ghost formations could equally be explained by natural means, such as visitors to crop circles trampling seed into the ground.

Ghost circles have also appeared in snow-covered fields, both in England and Holland. In one spectacular example, the circle which appeared at Oliver's Castle on 16th August 2008 (see picture p. 29) was visible again six months later when a light covering of snow lay on the ground, the snow having melted in the same patterns as the original formation. Hobby pilot Matthew Williams spotted this when he flew over on 8th January 2009 and took the photo on page 28. Towards the end of July 2009, the wheat crop was standing high again when once again the August 2008 formation was 'resurrected' as a ghost circle of darker coloured plants (see picture p. 30).

CHAPTER 2

THE CROP CIRCLE PHENOMENON FROM A HISTORICAL PERSPECTIVE

Opposite page: In July 2009, two circles appeared within a few days of each other close to Silbury Hill (Photo: Eva-Marie Brekkestø)

It's a widespread misunderstanding that the first crop circles appeared in England in the 1980s. The reason many people think this is probably that it was only then that the media really began to show any interest in the phenomenon. Not that crop circles had never been mentioned in the press before, but it wasn't until the end of the 1980s that the national newspapers, TV and radio began to feature reports of crop circles in England, which were soon picked up by the media in other countries.

It seems from the sources listed below, that crop formations before 1980 were usually just simple circles or rings, but not always. Even in the 19th and early 20th centuries, there were reports of squares, triangles and combinations of these which made up more complex patterns. As we shall see, in other places in the world such as South Africa, complex crop circle formations were noted long before corresponding patterns were confirmed in Europe. It's hard to know whether more advanced types of crop circles also appeared in other parts of the world in the previous centuries, as there was no opportunity in those times to see or photograph crop circles from the air.

Anyway, despite these cautions, it is still clear that the English crop circles went into a new phase of development from the mid-1980s. More of them appeared, or they began to be reported more systematically, or both, and the complexity of patterns developed dramatically, especially from 1990 onwards. In that year the circles, rings and quintuplets gave way to dumbbells and more linear patterns with various appendages, which were soon described as pictograms. The phenomenon took another new turn in 1991. On 17th July, at Barbury Castle, the first of a new type of formation appeared (see picture p.9), with several novel components and showing much more complex geometry than ever seen before. After that, although simple patterns continued to appear, there was a trend towards greater size and complexity, one which you could say culminated in July 2001 with the gigantic formation at Milk Hill [3] and the first of the two so-called 'alien faces' (about which more in chapter 7). The total numbers of formations recorded each year in the Crop Circle Connector archives have varied between 1988 and 2010 from 29 to 144, peaking in 1989 and 1999 and with dips in 1993 and 2006.

Since 2001 the patterns have maintained roughly the same level of complexity, but they never cease to surprise us. Beautiful corn circles with entirely new and original themes continue to emerge alongside reworkings of familiar design elements, and we marvel at a creativity which never seems to fade.

THE FIRST ENTHUSIASTS

At the beginning of the 1980s, Terence Meaden, Pat Delgado and Colin Andrews had begun to systematically report and record the appearance of crop circles in southern England. Andrews would become the most public figure out of these early researchers. His involvement started one July afternoon in 1983 when he was driving past Cheesefoot Head in Hampshire. Some patterns in a field by the side of the road caught his attention. More curious than the average motorist, Andrews stopped his car and got out to take a closer look. He found five circles in the field, in the shape

3 This crop formation, which appeared the night of 14th August 2001, was the biggest one we know of. It consisted of 409 circles, measured nearly 300 metres in diameter and covered an area equivalent to 10–12 football fields. See picture on page 194.

of a Celtic cross. Andrews, by training an electrical engineer, has described that event as if "a switch was thrown in my stomach". From that moment on, the crop circles became his great passion and they would come to play a pre-eminent role in his life.

Through the rest of the decade, Andrews and Delgado co-operated (at first with Meaden as well) to discover and catalogue more and more crop circles both in their home county of Hampshire and later with Busty Taylor in Wiltshire. At various times the formations they found got into the local news and onto regional TV, but it was when in 1989 Andrews and Delgado published the world's first book on the phenomenon, *Circular Evidence*, which was a huge success, that a lot more media attention was drawn to the subject. But by then Colin Andrews was already well known to the Wiltshire and Hampshire cereal farmers. His curiosity had led him to seek out any farmers who would talk to him and to ask them the same question: Had they ever seen crop circles before? What did they know about them? The answers were surprising. Many farmers told the same story: their parents, grandparents and great-grandparents had seen crop circles, and they had heard about them since they were children.

Robert Plot

THE FIRST WRITTEN SOURCES

In the years that followed, more and more stories of possible crop circles from long before the 1980s began to emerge or be tracked down by crop circle researchers such as Terry Wilson and Andreas Müller. In fact, we have written records suggesting crop circle appearances which go back as far as the 16th century. In 1590, the book *Daemonolatreia* was published by Nicholas Remy, an infamous trial judge during the Church's persecution of witches. In this guide to detecting witchcraft, Remy tells of an incident in the village of Assennuncuriam, then a part of Germany but now situated in Alsace Lorraine in France, where a group of women and men with cloven feet were found to be dancing in circles of flattened corn. Allowing for some exaggeration, at least about the feet, could it be that this anecdote reflects a history of veneration of crop circles by the 'wise women' of the time? (Müller 2001, Remigius 1590).

The first written sources for possible English crop circles date back to the late 17th century. Robert Plot was a naturalist and antiquarian who became the first professor of chemistry at the University of Oxford and the first keeper of the Ashmolean

Top: Plot's illustration of 'lightning' producing a 'fairy ring'.
Middle: crop circle at Barbury Castle in 1999
(Photo: Janet Ossebaard)
Bottom: the same field in 2000, when the corn grew more strongly
where the circle had been the previous year (Photo: Bert Janssen)

museum. In 1686 he published *A Natural History of Staffordshire*, in which he describes at some length the phenomenon of 'fairy rings'. He describes these as circles, often in groups of three or more, which appear "in arable grounds and open pastures". Plot says further that the circles can be up to 40 feet in diameter and that the earth in the circles is often dried out, a feature which many modern day crop circle researchers have noticed. In some cases deposits of "sulphur powder" have been found, Plot says.

In recent times, deposits of a white powder have been found in crop circles, most recently in Hoeven in the Netherlands in 2007 and 2009 and in three simple circles found at Honey Street, Wiltshire, on 4th July 2008. Plot further observed that where these 'fairy rings' had appeared, often there would be better growth in the following year's crop, something which has also often been reported from modern times, for example at Barbury Castle in 2000.

Plot includes in his booklet a special illustration of how he imagined the fairy rings to be created. The drawing shows a formation consisting of a square with a ring around it. In the sky we see black clouds from which emerge two trumpet-like tubes, pointing at the formation, one cylindrical and the other square in cross-section. Is Plot trying to show that an unusual weather phenomenon might create the rings? Plot concludes in fact that the agency is lightning. Theories that weather phenomena are responsible for crop circles have also been presented in modern times. We will return to those in chapter 4.

THE MOWING DEVIL

Perhaps the best known historical account, which has been retold in many crop circle books, is the story of the "The Mowing Devil" from 1678. This was first printed with an accompanying wood-cut illustration in a news pamphlet for the county of Hertfordshire. It was later reprinted in several compendiums and has been widely circulated since it was rediscovered in 1990, so that the different versions now going around have led some sceptics to dismiss the whole thing as an invention.

In 2005, determined to settle the matter once and for all, the well known crop circle researcher and author Andy Thomas took the trouble to chase the story back to its original sources. Thomas tracked down the last known surviving copy of the pamphlet in the British Library in London, and was able to confirm its existence. The eight-page pamphlet was yellowed and brittle but fully readable. Thomas realized that confusion had arisen because subsequent reprints in the 19th and 20th century had included some small editorial changes to the front cover, and the illustration appeared slightly different due to being copied by hand from the wood-cut, but the text was the same. The story is a Christian morality tale which describes how a rich farmer refuses to pay the asking price when he wants his field of oats to be cut. He dismisses the poor mower with a curse *"That the Devil himself should Mow his Oats before he [the mower] should have anything to do with them"*. The next night, the oat field is seen by the local villagers *"to be all of a Flame, and so continued for some space, to the great consternation of those that beheld it"*.

The farmer is told, and in the morning hurries to see the damage. But instead of being consumed by the 'flames', his oats have somehow been preserved after all. Naturally the work is attributed to the said Devil. The unknown author of the pamphlet describes the remarkable scene that greeted the farmer:

".. to his admiration he found the Crop was cut down ready to his hands; and [as] if the Devil had a mind to shew his dexterity in the art of Husbandry, and scorn'd to mow them after the usual manner, he cut them in round circles, and plac't every straw with that exactness that it would have taken up above an Age for any Man to perform what he did that one night".

Obviously there is one problem with connecting this description with the modern crop circle phenomenon, namely that the oats are clearly described as being mown, i.e. cut, rather than trampled or flattened. Indeed the illustration shows a cheeky-looking devil wielding a scythe. However, other factors speak strongly in its favour: the mention of 'round (concentric?) circles', the admiration of the neatness and precision of the job, and the idea that the supposed Devil's handiwork would have been impossible for human hands to accomplish in one night. The field in flames could well have been a way of describing some of the strange light phenomena often associated with the formation of crop circles (which we will return to in chapter 3), especially if the villagers didn't dare go too close. And the wood-cut illustration, appealing though it is, is unlikely to have been done by an eye-witness but rather to have been commissioned later by the publisher.

An appreciation of the literary context of this pamphlet also lends support to the

The original version of The Mowing Devil, which was printed in the Hertfordshire news pamphlet from 1678

conviction that this is our oldest known written English crop circle account. Much of the pamphlet, typical of its time and its genre, is taken up with driving home the moral of how worldly wealth bears with it social responsibilities - and spiritual penalties for the undeserving[4]. The author is not concerned with the details of the putative crop circle - perhaps not even whether the oats were cut or laid - except insofar as they emphasize the physical existence and the power of the Devil as a warning to the impious. In a purely fictional account, the farmer could easily have been punished by having his oats burnt to a cinder by the devil's flames. Instead they are beautifully cut and laid 'ready to his hands'. The farmer's punishment is more subtle, for now he is humbled and chastened by the results of his arrogant curse. The story concludes:

"And the man that owns them is as yet afraid to remove them."

EARLY REPORTS

In earlier times, as mentioned, crop circles were a known phenomenon both in England and other countries. Since 1950 there have been so many crop circle reports that it would be impossible to list them all in this book, but they are detailed in full in Terry Wilson's book *The Secret History of Crop Circles* (Wilson 1998). From the 1950s to the end of the 1980s, formations were reported from Great Britain, Sweden, Romania, Switzerland, France, the Netherlands, Russia, the USA, Canada, Mexico, Hawaii, Argentina, Brazil, Uruguay, Nigeria, Kenya, New Zealand, Australia and Japan. The lists below show how well documented the crop circle phenomenon was even before 1950.

GREAT BRITAIN

- 1830: East Anglia: circle reported in a letter to the Sunday Mirror newspaper (Svahn 1998).
- 1871: Plummer's Hill, High Wycombe, Buckinghamshire: on the 4th October, the day after an observation of a 'star-like object' in the same area, William Loosley

---

4 See full text at http://ufologie.net7htm/mowingdevil.htm

reported finding a simple circle of flattened grass and weeds (Loosley 1979.

- 1880: Guildown, Surrey: several circles in wheat. Reported by J. Rand Capron. See below for more details (Capron 1880).
- 1890s: Thurso, Scotland: several circles in corn. Reported by Jean Songhurst (Randles and Fuller 1993).
- 1900–1910: Tilshead, Wiltshire: six circles (four large and two smaller) in wheat. Reported by Constance Wheeler (Fuller and Rendall 1994).
- 1914–1956: Maiden Bradley, Wiltshire: several circles in corn. Reported by C.L. Dutton, who stated that her family had been seeing crop circles in the same area since the middle of the 19th century (Fuller and Rendall 1994)
- 1918: Billington, Kent: Large circle in oats. Reported by Joan Tookey (Meaden 1991(1)).
- 1922: Chilcomb, Hampshire: simple circle in corn (CPR, Andrews).
- 1924: Devizes, Wiltshire: several circles in corn. Reported by Teddy Wheeler (Fuller and Rendall 1994).
- 1927 or 1928, July: Chanctonbury, West Sussex: circle in grass. Reported by Roger Sear (Delgado, CPR Newsletter nr. 3, 1991).
- 1930: Burghwallis, South Yorkshire: triangular formation in corn (McCormack and Horn 1994).
- 1932: Bow Hill, West Sussex: a ring in corn. Periodical article with photograph (Curven 1936–1937).
- 1935: Helions Bumpstead, Essex: Two simple circles in wheat and maize. Reported by Paul Germany, who witnessed the circles form (*Sunday Express* 12.8.1990 in Fuller and Rendall 1989).
- 1937: Helions Bumpstead, Essex: Three circles in corn. Reported by Paul Germany, who witnessed the first one form (Randles andFuller 1993).
- 1939: Kilmacanogue, Scotland: a circle in reeds, ten metres in diameter (Svahn 1998, p. 174).
- 1940 or 1941, August: Leicestershire, Earl Shilton: three circles in wheat, reported by a Mr. Lawrence (Randles and Fuller 1990).
- 1940s: Mill End, Hertfordshire: pattern of three circles with 10cm wide curving corridors. Later: several simple circles. Reported by a Mrs. Staermose (Wilson 1998).
- 1940s: Kingham, Oxfordshire: several circles in corn, reported by Gwen Horrigan

(Andrews and Delgado 1989).

- 1940s: Abergavenny, Wales: several circles (Svahn 1998, p. 174).
- 1940s: Elton, Cheshire: several simple circles (Fortean Times issue nr. 62 referred to in Wilson 1998).
- 1940s: Cilycwm, Camarthenshire: simple circle in wheat, reported by W. C. Williams who watched the circle being formed (Fuller and Rendall 1992).
- 1943, July: Fylde, Lancashire: several circles with a spiral lay (Fuller and Rendall 1992).
- 1943: Tangmere, West Sussex: two circles in corn (Thomas 1996).
- 1945: Chilcomb, Hampshire: two circles (CPR, Andrews).
- 1946 and subsequently: Cheriton, Hampshire: a number of circles and formations in corn (Wilson 1998).
- 1946: Ivinghoe Aston, Buckinghamshire: circle in barley, 35 metres in diameter (Fuller and Rendall 1992).
- 1947: Pilling, Lancashire: simple circle in potato plants, 45 metres in diameter. Reported by John Salisbury (*Crop Watcher* nr. 7 referred to in Wilson 1998).

OTHER COUNTRIES

- 1860–1870: Germany, Nordrhein-Westfalen, Niederzier: several circles in grass and corn. Reported by a Mr Reuter (Müller 2001, p.12).
- early 1900s, before 1910: India, Panchgani: large circle surrounded by nine smaller ones (Crop Circle Archive).
- early 1900s, before 1910: India, Panchgani: simple circle (Crop Circle Archive).
- early 1900s, before 1910: Australia, Adelaide: triangle with a single circle in the centre and a circle at each corner (Crop Circle Archive).
- early 1900s, before 1910: Australia, Adelaide: triangle surrounded by two concentric rings (Crop Circle Archive).
- 1927: Australia, New South Wales, Fernvale: Unknown pattern (Crop Circle Archive).
- 1930: Ireland, Co. Donegal: several circles in corn. Reported by Jean Songhurst (Randles and Fuller 1993).
- 1933: Netherlands, Noord Brabant: simple circle in corn (Paul Fuller's archive, ref. Wilson 1998).
- 1938: Belgium, Overboelare: numerous circles in corn, probably forming a

complex pattern. Reported by Marcel Van Nieuwenhoeve (Randles and Fuller 1993).

- 1939: Ireland, Kilmacanogue: circle in reeds, 10 metres in diameter (Randles and Fuller 1990).
- 1941: USA, Ohio, Middeltown: simple circle (Fuller and Rendall 1993).
- 1946: Germany, Welspang, Schleswig-Holstein: five circles in cornfield. Reported by H. Lagies, who saw the circles forming (Müller 2001).
- 1949: South Africa, Natal: three adjacent circles in a potato field. Reported by Credo Mutwa (Müller 2005).
- 1950: Kenya: Several circles in a cornfield seen by a Mrs. Brown (Müller 2005).
- 1950: Norway, Hedmark, Stange: three circles in cornfield. Seen by S.A. Aaby (author's interview with witness 2008).

Some of the crop circles mentioned above are worthy of closer study:

Surrey in 1880
Meteorologist Peter Van Doorn discovered an interesting article in the scientific periodical Nature for 1880. It describes circles of flattened corn in a way which anyone who has visited a crop circle today will recognize:

J. Rand Capron, a naturalist and amateur scientist living in Guildown in Surrey, tells how after a short thunderstorm on 21st July 1880 he went to visit a neighbouring farmer. He found the farmer out in his wheat field looking at some circles of flattened corn. Together they investigated the formations more closely and Capron noticed that in the centre of all the circles there were some stems of corn still standing. Around the centres, the corn was laid neatly and in one direction only. The standing plants at the edges of the circles made an even, circular wall. Capron described the crop as healthy, with strong stems, and concluded that the phenomenon was caused by a whirlwind of some sort (Capron 1880).

Early observations of crop circles and UFOs in the USA
In the 1880s, on a farm in Oskaloosa, Mahaska County, Iowa, a family witnessed a flying object that was 'lit up like a birthday cake'. The object proceeded to fly over them until they lost sight of it behind a nearby hill, whereupon they retreated to their

storm cellar for the night. The next day they found a large circle in the grass field behind the hill with several burned areas. Several neighbours also reported seeing the object in the air. (ICCRA (2)).

Around 10:00 a.m. on June the 3rd 1920, in Mount Pleasant, Henry County, Iowa an eyewitness saw a 'shiny-blue translucent egg-shaped' object 'the size of a fire hydrant' fly out of the sky and land silently about 15 feet away from him near a riverbank. It sat quietly for about 15 minutes before flying slowly away. A single, flattened circle in the grass was found where the object had sat (Fuller and Rendall 1993).

Sussex 1932: first English report with a photograph
The first photograph of an alleged crop circle in England was tracked down by Andreas Müller. In a newsletter of the Sussex Archaeological Society from 1932 he found an article about a ring of flattened barley in a field on the Chichester Downs, complete with photograph (see illustration p.43):

The author of the article, E. Cecil Curwen, was out for a walk on Bow Hill north-west of Chichester, when some passers-by told pointed out to him some rings in a cornfield on nearby Stoughton Down. Curwen judged the rings to be about 40 metres in diameter. When he went closer to take a look at the rings, it turned out that only one of them consisted of flattened barley, while the other three could not be seen on the ground (Sussex Notes and Queries 1932).

As well as the photograph, the article includes a detailed report and a sketch of the rings. Comparing the sketch with the photo, it looks as if the light areas in the background correspond with the positions of the other rings. Müller suggests that these are probably crop marks from archaeological remains previously ploughed out by the farmer (www.cropcirclescience.org).

Wales 1941
In 2005 a Mr. Barry Smith contributed the following account to the BBC's web archive of World War 2 memories:
"During WW2 I was evacuated to Wales from Birmingham as it was being heavily bombed. I lived on a farm in the village of Arddleen near Llanymynech.

One day in the late summer of 1941 I was given a good hiding by the farmer's grown up son for allegedly damaging the corn. (Damage to food crops was very serious then as food was in short supply and rationed). I was taken to see two corn circles I was supposed to have made. They were some way in to the field and could only be seen by standing on the field gate. A typical five-barred farm gate. They were about 15 metres in diameter. I did not make them and we never found out who did. Was I blamed for some of the earliest corn circles?" (WW2 Peoples war).

Norway 1950

In December 2008 the author visited a goldsmith in Oslo, Norway, in order to have a crop circle pendant, bought in England, refashioned into a brooch. Mrs Aaby, who knew nothing about the English crop circles, stared in fascination at the design and asked what it represented. After hearing the whole story about the modern crop circle phenomenon, she was silent for a while and appeared deeply touched, then began talking about something she had witnessed as a child, but had apparently remained silent about ever since, for fear of ridicule. The author later recorded the story as follows:

Late in August 1950 I was staying at Sørum farm at Stange in the county of Hedmark. I was with my father and a young farm worker out in the fields. It was hard to get hold of agricultural machinery so soon after the war. They had borrowed a combine harvester and were going to try it out, when we found the formation. It consisted of three circles of flattened corn. Two of the circles were about one and a half metres in diameter (when I lay down in them, I could just reach the edges with my arms outstretched), and the third was about three times as big. I remember thinking that the circles were placed roughly like the head and feet of a man. I remember also that my father wasn't surprised by the discovery. He explained to me that these were "field rings" or "field circles" and talked about them as a known phenomenon. The circles were perfectly round, the stems were laid down evenly and neatly and the corn lay in beautiful swirls around the centre of each circle. I was only six years old when this happened, but the event is still clear in my memory.

First known photo of a crop circle, published in an archaeological journal (Sussex Notes and Queries 1932)

This report is interesting because it suggests that crop circles were already a known phenomenon in at least this part of Norway in the 1950s. The fact that the farmer had a name for them implies that it wasn't the first time he or his family had come across such a thing.

Germany

The earliest indication of possible crop circles in Germany is from West Holstein in 1959. An aerial photograph of an oil refinery at Dithmarsch shows dozens of circular patterns, irregularly distributed and of different sizes, in the fields around. There are many irregular patches of what appears to be flattened crop or grass, but also a number of cleanly cut out circular patches (Müller 2001).

Reed circles in Australia

On the 19th January 1966, not far from the small town of Tully, near Cairns in Northern Queensland, farm worker George Pedley was driving his tractor along the track that led to a banana plantation when he heard a strange, hissing sound. At first he thought that air was escaping from a tractor tyre, but when the hissing got so loud that it drowned out the tractor's engine noise, he started looking around to see what it could be. About 40 metres away, he caught sight of a flying object rising above the tree tops. Pedley described the object as bluish grey in colour, looking like two saucers stuck together, and guessed that it was around 8 metres in diameter. It dipped towards the ground briefly before shooting off at great speed and disappearing. Pedley assumed that the unknown object had risen from the marshy area underneath, which is known as Horseshoe Lagoon. The water in the lagoon at the time of the incident was about 2 metres deep, but was largely obscured by dense vegetation described as consisting of rushes or swamp grass. When Pedley drove around a bend in the track to the lagoon, there was a round, flattened depression in the swamp grass about 8 to 10 metres in diameter. After bringing the landowner and other locals to see the strange phenomenon, Pedley reported the incident to the local police, and the next day Sergeant V.A. Moylan made the first of several visits to the site. His report confirmed Pedley's description and stated that there were no signs of any tracks into the lagoon whether of human beings or animals.

After the story made front page news in local and national newspapers, many other reports started to come in of 'UFO nests' in the Tully area as well as of UFO sightings, though not linked together in the way the first one was. For example, farmer Tom Warren and schoolmaster Hank Penning were walking around Horseshoe Lagoon a few days later when they found two more circular depressions in the reeds, only 25 metres from the one Pedley had found but hidden by dense vegetation. These circles were only two and a half metres in diameter. One looked fresh and new, while the other looked older and more withered. The reeds in both circles were laid in anticlockwise swirls. (Magee 1966).

Crop circles in Africa

Credo Mutwa is a well known Zulu spiritual leader and shaman who was born in Natal province in 1921. His mother was also a healer within the Zulu tradition, while his father was a Christian and a Catholic. Mutwa grew up with both a native African and a western-style education at local mission schools. Mutwa was later chosen as high leader of 500 traditional shamans and healers. In his book *Isilwane (The Animal: tales and fables from Africa)*, Mutwa writes the following about crop circles in his homeland:

At harvest time, we left some of our corn standing so that passing birds could share in the bounty of our fields and, by sharing, bless us and ensure us of plenty of food. Sometimes large fields of corn and millet were planted. These were sacred to the goddess and were offered to the vast armies of birds to eat. No human being could enter the sacred cornfield. The sacred fields were ploughed far from the ordinary millet, maize and corn, as they were left unfenced. Over centuries, people had discovered that the star gods sometimes communicated with human beings through these sacred fields. Time and again, strange circular depressions were seen in the centre of these fields. These depressions were called "Izishoze Zamatongo", the great circles of the gods.

These circles were an amazing sight to see. The gods never cut the stalks of corn or millet when they form these depressions. It appears as though a great circular, disk-shaped force has descended on the field. It pressed the corn firmly into the ground, without breaking the stalks or damaging the plants. Then the force appears to spin, resulting in the strange spiral appearance of the fallen stalks. Words cannot describe such a phenomenon, which I have seen more than thirty times in the course of my life as a traditional healer. Whenever a circle appeared

Top: One of the reed circles in Tully, Australia 1966
(Photo: P.V. Vignale)
Above: Credo Mutwa

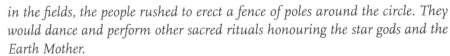

in the fields, the people rushed to erect a fence of poles around the circle. They would dance and perform other sacred rituals honouring the star gods and the Earth Mother.

All the kings and chiefs awaited the arrival of these circles. The appearance would be cause for celebrations that lasted several days. These celebrations were accompanied by prayers to the gods to watch over the people and to talk to them through the sacred circles (Mutwa 1996).

In 2005 Andreas Müller travelled to South Africa to meet Mutwa, then aged 84. We reproduce here some interesting extracts from the interview that followed:

I have seen hundreds of crop circles in my lifetime.
What you call 'Crop Circles' is the same (as) what the Zulu call 'Izishoze Zamatongo' and which means the designs or the writings of the gods. We have known about them for more than 4000 years.

I saw my very first crop circle in the Natal region in 1949. It was made of three circles inside each other placed in a field of potato plants. In 1958, again in Natal I saw a huge crop circle in the shape of two circles inside of a triangle.

On farms in Botswana there appeared a number of crop circles – many of them. I was called to go there and that was in 1959. I remember these were on sand and they were on the millet.

In the same year when I visited England and saw the large threefold Galaxy crop circle [5] near Avebury. I also visited a beautiful one in the Eastern Transvaal. It showed a symmetrical pattern inside a ring made of two crescents and inside of each a five-pointed star.

When asked by Müller, Mutwa sketched three crop circles he had seen.
He continued:
Our modern minds have been corrupted by western civilisation that is refusing to believe that things like the crop circles could be real and important. This is why we do not understand the simple messages any more.

———

5   The Triple Julia-Set crop circle which appeared next to Windmill Hill 7th July 1996.

The crop circles also tell us about the situation of the Sun. But why - you may ask – is the Earth Mind telling us about the Sun? The crop circle phenomenon talks of a time of great activity of the sun. But why? Why does this great intelligence, this Mother Spirit, why does it tell us about this thing? When there is trouble in the sun – then what happens to the human beings down here? When there is trouble in the sun there will be also trouble down on earth. And this is why the crop circles are appearing. They even tell us things that will happen in the future. They can also be warnings. For example if there is going to be a war – the crop circles tell us.

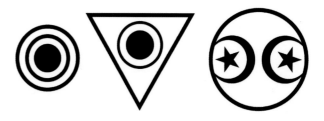

Andreas Müller's re-drawing of Credo Mutwa's sketches of three South African corn circles.

In the old days, when the Gods put crop circles in our fields the people used to run quickly to take sticks and stones all around the design to mark it out. We wanted that the Gods should say again what they are telling us. This is therefore so that the crop circle does not die and that the Gods will then again respond with another crop circle nearby. This is why sometimes there will be a new crop circle next to an old one.

This is how the African stone circle monuments came into existence. And this happened all over the worldwide as with Stonehenge, Avebury and the like. The Stonehenge monument you can see today, there used to be a crop circle there. This would have been regarded as a very holy thing so the ancient people marked it with earth, stones and wooden sticks. They are a sort of saying 'Thank you' to the intelligence that is behind.

I remember that my grandmother used to say that we must show respect for the crop circles as well as we have to show our respect to the standing stones.

We also find crop circles in the African grass or in the African savannah like in Kenya where there is a lot of good grass. If you want to see good crop circles – go to Kenya. In Masai Mara where the animals run plenty. You will see circles in the grass there – just as beautiful as these (pointing to the picture section of Müller's book).

Mutwa's mention of crop circles in Kenya is supported by English crop circle researcher Allan Brown, whose mother grew up on a farm outside Nairobi in the 1950s. She remembers how as a child she used to play in circles of flattened corn on the family farm (Andreas Müller, pers. comm.).

CROP CIRCLES IN FOLK LORE AND LEGEND

In *Thirty Indian Legends of Canada*, published in 1992 by Margaret Bemister, we find the story "The daughters of the stars", which tells of a hunter who discovers a strange circle in the prairie grass:

It looked as if people had run around in a ring until the grass was trampled down. As he could see no marks of footsteps leading away from the ring, he wondered very much whose feet could have marked out the circle. Then he made up his mind to hide, so that he might see if any one came.

After a while, he heard the sound of beautiful music. It seemed to come from the sky. As he looked up he saw something coming down through the air, and the music sounded like the singing of girls. As the object came closer, he saw that it was a wicker basket, and in it were twelve beautiful maidens. When the basket reached the ground, they all jumped out and began to dance around the circle... But as soon as the maidens saw the figure of a man, they ran to the basket, jumped in, and were at once drawn up to the sky (Bemister 1992).

Recent research has thrown new light onto the history of the crop circle phenomenon by uncovering references to possible crop circles within some classic European folk tales. The Brothers Grimm, for example, re-tell a fairy tale from Ireland which features rings supposedly made by fairies (*Irische Elfenmärchen*). In other works, the Brothers Grimm are careful to distinguish between 'witches' rings' (Hexenringe), which are rings of lush grass growth where certain species of mushroom have spread in a circular pattern, and 'fairy rings' (Elfenringe), which are circles of flattened plants trampled by the feet of fairies dancing around in the fields by night.

British folk lore often mentions 'fairy rings', however these are usually involving mushrooms, but interestingly the Grimm brothers include some of the 'Celtic' parts of Britain in the distribution pattern of their 'elven rings': "Circles trampled in the dewy grass occur in Scotland, Northern Germany and Scandinavia, and everyone cries, "Here the fairies have been dancing! On the Isle of Man they have even found tracks in the snow from their dancing feet" (Grimm 1826).

The German poet Heinrich Heine writes in his book *Elementargeister* (Nature spirits): *Dancing is characteristic of air spirits. They are such etheric beings, but still, delicate though they are, where they have danced a nightly round, their little feet still leave traces in the grass. These are the flattened circles known as 'fairy rings' (Elfenringe).* (Heine 1837).

One famous tale recorded by the Brothers Grimm is called 'The Twelve Swans'. The story actually begins with a farmer finding a circle of flattened corn in his field one morning. The circle seemed to have been made by tiny, delicate feet. Anxious to discover who could have made the circle, the farmer's two eldest sons keep watch the first and second nights, but without success, for they both give up on account of violent thunderstorms. On the third night, the youngest son Hans manages to stick it out and is rewarded by the sight of twelve swans landing in the cornfield. The swans take off their swan feathers and transform themselves into young maidens who then begin to dance in such a way that the corn is bent down. The crop circle theme doesn't reappear after that, and after various setbacks the story ends with Hans marrying one of the swan maidens.

Paintings of semi-naked fairies dancing in rings were a popular theme of Victorian painters in both Britain and in Scandinavia, where they are known as 'fairy dances' or 'elven dances'. In his research, Andreas Müller came across a reference to a Scandinavian tale which describes 'fairy dances'. On Müller's request, and with the help of my local library, I managed to track down the book En Krönika om Åsbro (A chronicle of Åsbro), a collection of folk tales from Örebro (a Swedish county to the west of Stockholm). In the book, the author AnneMarie Hellström quotes from a 1926 account by August Isaksson, recorded by Gustav Olsson in Ulma:

'The fairies' dance' by the Swedish painter Nils Blommér

On the shores of the lake, where the trees grow close to the water, one could find the places where fairies go to dance. These were circular spots where the grass was flattened down as smooth as a floor. They were made by the fairies dancing there. I saw one of these by Lake Tisar. They could be dangerous, one could get sick if one walked in such a place or disturbed anything there (Hellström 1990).

On the basis of the historical documentation, we can conclude that the crop circle phenomenon goes back much further in time than the sceptics would have us believe. On the one hand, it is clear that crop circles have featured in European, Native American and African folklore in earlier centuries. On the other, reputable scientists during the same period have also taken note of the phenomenon. In other words, crop circles were known about and discussed long before the English and international media began to make a fuss about them at the beginning of the 1990s!

CHAPTER 3

EYEWITNESS REPORTS

Facing page: Crop formation with interference pattern, Aldbourne July 2005 (Photo: Terje Toftenes)

Over the years, quite a few people have witnessed crop circles forming, in several different countries. I here define 'crop circle' as a (most often) circular area of plants that are flattened in a precise way. What follows is an overview of the best known accounts, some sketchy and some more detailed. Some eyewitnesses have seen whirlwinds seemingly producing circles of downed corn, some witnesses speak of strange lights or even structured craft hovering over the site where the plants are flattened, and in some cases the witnesses don't mention any causative agents. Many of the reports were written down before the concept of 'crop circles' as such evolved in the 1980s, and therefore do not use those words. Some witnesses describe incidents where they actually saw the corn going down. Other observations are of unusual light and wind phenomena at places where crop circles have been discovered very soon afterwards. The third category includes cases where witnesses could confirm that crop circles had formed within a short space of time.

DIRECT WITNESSES TO CROP CIRCLES FORMING

1934 EVERSDEN, CAMBRIDGESHIRE

This eye witness account of a 'crop circle' being formed by a whirlwind was first recorded in August 1990, when the Sunday Express newspaper printed a letter to

the editor from Kathleen Skin of Cambridgeshire. Later Miss Skin was interviewed by the crop circle researcher Terence Meaden, who printed the full story in his book "Circles in the Sky" in 1991. The following is extracted from Meaden's book:

It was an afternoon in late July 1934 when Kathleen Skin, then 14 years old, witnessed a crop circle being formed. The place was Eversden, ten kilometres from Cambridge. Kathleen was seated in the shade of a hedgerow facing a five-acre wheat field. It was a hot, dry, sultry, windless day, and there was nothing to be seen in the sky – no wind, and no sound. While she was sitting there the farmer, Mr. Hagger, stopped to chat before he moved on. She was gazing over a wheat field waiting to be harvested, when suddenly she heard a crackling like fire and saw a whirlwind in the centre of the field forming a circle in the corn. The whirlwind was spinning stalks, seeds and dust up into the air for about 100 or more feet. She started running towards it, but within seconds it had left its circle and was traversing the field. She reached the circle to find a perfect circle of flattened corn, the stalks lying clockwise, interlaced and their ears lying on top of each another (some even plaited) on the periphery. The air in the circle seemed hot and she could fell the warmth of the corn through her shoes. She touched the lying wheat with her hand and was amazed at how hot the fallen crop was, too hot to touch.

By this time the whirlwind had reached the corner of the field and created a second circle about four metres in diameter. Kathleen did not enter the circle, but went home to tell her mother about it. She went back the next day and found the farmer harvesting the field. He had seen such circles before, he said, adding that the circle was nothing unusual and that it was locally known that whirlwinds were able to make such circles in the crops (Meaden 1991 (2), p. 179).

1935 HELIONS BUMPSTEAD, ESSEX

During 1991 & 1992 the Sunday Mirror newspaper ran a competition to find the cause of the crop circles. One reader who wrote to the newspaper was Paul Germany from Suffolk, who described seeing a crop circle form when he was ten years old in 1935:

I was working in the harvest fields on the Suffolk-Essex border, during a pause in our labours I happened to be looking at wheat field about 400m away and saw a crop circle form. "What's that?" I said to my companion, he replied, "You do not want to worry about them, boy you often see them – the old men used to call them Devil's twists…". The farmer gave me a pitch fork and told me to raise the fallen corn. I stood in the circle but I faced a futile task, as fast as I raised the corn stalks they sprang back into place (Randles and Fuller 1993, p. 224).

In the same letter mentioned in the report above, Paul Germany also remembered a later incident when he saw a linear triplet form at the same location:

1937 HELIONS BUMPSTEAD, ESSEX

About 7.00 am the wind began to increase and swirl around. I paused and just happened to be looking across a shallow valley to the opposite side, the first crop ring appeared, then another and a third. After so many years I cannot be precise about the time interval between successive rings but I think it was about four seconds, and the spacing between rings 1 and 2 was 100m, between 2 and 3, 80m – all in a straight line" (Randles and Fuller 1993, p. 224).

The Sunday Mirror competition produced several other eyewitness accounts. For example, Bill Williams of Gloucestershire recalled seeing several crop circles on his father's farm at Cilycwm, Dyfed in the late 1940s:

LATE 1940S, CILYCWM, CAMARTHENSHIRE, WALES

"With reference to the corn circles mystery, I actually witnessed one being made. I was standing in a cornfield one morning and saw a whirlwind touching the ground and forming a circle in the corn. It was just the strength of the wind in the whirlwind that formed the circle".

Terence Meaden later interviewed Mr Williams and got some more details from him. The event happened in the late 1940s when Mr Williams was working on his father's farm, Penfedw Farm at Cilycwm near Llandovery. He was then in his twenties. The area is surrounded by hills on all sides, and circles had been seen there "frequently". On this occasion, a weekday in August, at about 10.30 to 11 in the morning, Mr Williams had gone into the wheat field on harvesting day in advance of the cutting and binding machinery, and was crossing the middle of the field when he heard the buzzing noise of a whirlwind starting up only a few metres away. According to Meaden, Williams then saw a spinning mass of air with dust in it, and, as he watched, in a matter of *"only a couple of seconds or so, the wheat fell down producing a hard-edged circle 3 to 4 metres in diameter"*. It looked just like other crop circles he had seen before except that this one was completely flat-bottomed whereas some of the earlier ones had stalks standing at their centres like a conical pyramid. The vortex then died out rapidly, but during its brief lifetime (under 4 or 5 seconds) it remained at the same place (Meaden 1991, p. 199 (I)).

1937 HELIONS BUMPSTEAD, ESSEX, ENGLAND

In 1946 Henning Lagies was an eleven-year old boy living with his mother's family in Angeln, an area of Schleswig-Holstein in north Germany. The following describes his experience in his own words, according to a report made by Andreas Müller:

One day, in the summer of '46, I had struck out from Wellspang to Süderfahrenstedt on an errand; I had taken the paved road leading north to Böklund to the top of the rise about one kilometre north of Wellspang, where a dirt road branched off to the left to Süderfahrenstedt. It was a pleasantly warm day, not a cloud in the sky, and, probably most significantly, not even the slightest breeze blowing. As I walked along that dirt road, I came to a section of fields slightly elevated above the surrounding area. Suddenly I became aware of a faint whistling sound and a gentle swaying of the hazelnut, sloe, and elder bushes growing on the hedgerows along both sides of the road. Then, about twenty-five metres to my left, I noticed a three metre wide column of plant debris spiralling counter-clockwise upward to a height of, initially, about eighteen metres. A second or two later four smaller columns arose at ninety degree intervals around the central spiral, each about one and a half metres wide and spaced approximately two metres, edge to edge, from the main column, and, I am quite certain of this, spinning clockwise. The one at the left rear from my position collapsed very quickly, but the other three rose rapidly and caught up with the central column at about eighteen metres. At that height the tops of all four started to whip around violently, and, as they contacted each other, they dissolved into a single turbulent and widening column that kept rising at a perceived angle of about twenty degrees from the vertical to my right to a height of at least eighty metres; at that height the debris became too faint to be visible.
By this time a brisk wind was blowing in the direction of the disturbance – presumably from all directions. I made my way through the crop, I think it was oats, to investigate, and I found one large and three smaller sharply defined circles, of the same diameters and directions of rotation of the downed stalk as their respective debris columns, each with a central cone of stalks wrapped loosely around

each other. The collapsed spiral had left only a very faint trace (Müller 2001, p. 55).

A report from the Centre for Crop Circle Studies database describes an event in southern England in 1950. About 10 o'clock one night in July, Mr. E. Perrett was with his father when they witnessed 'whirlwinds' creating a circle in a field of corn. The stems were bent over in a clockwise swirl (Wilson 1998, p. 145).

1950 HASLEMERE, SURREY

On the night of 19th August a scoutmaster was driving some boys home after a meeting when he saw glowing lights in some thick bushes. The scoutmaster stopped his car and walked to a nearby clearing where he saw a strange object in the sky. Although made unconscious by the experience he remembered a dome-shaped UFO hovering just over the ground and leaving behind a circle of flattened grass. The incident was investigated by Captain Edward Ruppelt in the US Air Force and is included in the Project Blue Book (Randles and Fuller 1990, p.157).

1952 WEST PALM BEACH, FLORIDA, USA

Numerous witnesses observed a UFO at a distance of less than 20m. When it flew away, it left a flattened circle in a field of corn. The circle subsequently yielded no plant growth (Fuller and Rendall 1993).

1954 MEXICO

At about 10pm on the evening of 14th October 1958, two men (Harry Sjöberg and Stig Ekberg) were driving along an empty road towards Väddö north of the town of Norrtälje. As they were approaching Söderäng, the headlights in their car started to fade and the engine spluttered. Stig noticed a bright star in the sky, which then grew bigger as it got closer. As the UFO descended towards the road, its light illuminated the roadside vegetation and the surroundings. The object went in to land about 100m in front of the car, which had now come to a stop. The men could now see a silvery-coloured craft about 8m long and 3 to 4m high, rotating slowly just above the ground. They could see hot air moving under the UFO and shimmering in different colours. After about ten minutes the UFO took off again and disappeared. The men started the car and drove on to the spot where it has been hovering. In the light of the car headlights they could see that the grass on the side of the road was pressed down in a semicircle. Taking a closer look at the road, they found a shiny piece of metal, triangular and with rounded edges. It was warm to the touch and unusually heavy for its size (Svahn 1998, pp. 55–70).

1958 VÄDDÖ, UPPLAND, SWEDEN

1960 KENYA

A number of witnesses saw a crop circle appear in a sugar cane field. Accompanied by a tremendous noise. (Fuller and Rendall 1992).

1962 SWAYFIELD BRIDGE, LINCOLNSHIRE

In an article in Steam World in September 1990, train-spotter Noel Ingram recalls an incident which took place at 6.40 pm on 7 June 1962 near Swayfield Bridge in Lincolnshire, as he was sitting waiting for the east coast Pullman express to pass by.

I was enjoying the countryside between trains when there was a sudden roaring in the crop field to the left [of the railway line]. A sudden whirlwind whipped up the crop skyward and then stopped as suddenly as it had begun – leaving behind a ring of flattened crop! I was too startled to use the camera hanging around my neck (Randles and Fuller 1993, p. 222).

1964 HUBBARD, OREGON, USA

At 7.30 am on 18th May 1964, 10-year-old Michael Bizon observed a square, 3m long, 1.5 m high silvery object with a cone-shaped front part, resting on four shining legs in a wheat field. It made a 'beep' and issued a smell like gas fumes as it took off. It first rose to the height of the telephone poles and then took off vertically. When Bizon inspected the field he found three circles of flattened wheat about one metre in diameter and approximately one metre apart from one another, forming an equilateral triangle (Randles and Fuller 1990, p. 159).

1966 DOVER, KENT

Mr. R. Roberts reported the formation of a circle in grass by a bizarre agency which resembled a translucent blue tube. The tube sealed off the grass, and rain was deflected by it, with loud hissing sounds taking place at the same time. A great disturbance in the air was also reported, and nearby livestock was seemingly transfixed (Fuller and Rendall 1992).

1966 BRISBANE, AUSTRALIA

A single circle approx 28 feet (9m) in diameter was discovered in the grass in the spot beneath where a school teacher and class of children witnessed a silver UFO (Fuller and Rendall 1991).

1968 HILL RIVER, AUSTRALIA

Facing page:
Crop circle at West Kennet Long Barrow, June 2008 (Photo: Gary King)

Two children watched a 60 cm long by 25 cm thick football-shaped luminous object, golden in colour, pass within fifty metres of them and appear to land in a paddock. A spot was later found flattened in an oval shape 150 cm long. It was "tangled in a

corkscrew fashion as if a giant top had spun on the spot" (Pix-People Magazine 1972).

1969 IBIUNA, BRAZIL

At 2 am. on the 17th June, a man and his wife saw a bright oval object, glowing 'like a mercury lamp'. It hovered for 45 minutes, projecting a beam of light into the trees, then vanished. The next day they returned and found an 8m diameter circle of flattened vegetation, found swirled anti-clockwise (Randles and Fuller 1990, p. 160).

1972 WARMINSTER, WILTSHIRE, ENGLAND

The night of August 12th 1972, Bryce Bond went into a field of wheat when he became engulfed in coloured lights, and heard reassuring voices in his head. He continues:

Suddenly, I heard a noise - like something crushing the wheat down (...) and there before my eyes, a large depression was being formed. The wheat was being crushed down in a counter-clockwise position. It too was shaped like a triangle and measured about twenty feet (6 metres) from point to point (Shuttlewood 1996).

1974 LANGENBURG, SASKATCHEWAN, CANADA

At 11 am. Edwin Fuhr was on his swather in a field of rapeseed. Moving up a small incline, he glanced up to make sure he would skirt a grassy, dried out slough just ahead when he spied something made of metal in the grass. His first thought was that someone was playing a joke on him or had dumped junk in the old slough. As the swather moved up the incline, the slough came into full view. The metallic 'something' was one of five machines rotating rapidly and hovering just above the grass. Fuhr, startled, stopped his swather, climbed down and took a few steps toward the hovering machines. Then, overcome with fear, he stopped and began slowly to ease back to his idling swather. The machines continued to hover and spin, then slowly lifted. About 100 feet above ground, they manoeuvred into an echelon formation and rose at a much greater speed. Each vented a brief puff of smoke and in seconds they disappeared over the horizon. At the controls of his swather, Fuhr was almost paralysed with fright and barely able to put the machine into gear. At lunch, he was unable to eat. When he inspected the site where the strange visitors had been, he saw five circular depressions. Most of the tall grass was pressed down, and, in places, was twisted as it would be by a spinning object. The circles were exactly 11 feet (3.3 meters) in diameter and there was unflattened grass in the centre. (Andrews and Delgado 1989, p. 183).

During the night of 8th December, a woman and her daughter heard a strange noise and found two areas of strawberry plants, flattened in an anti-clockwise direction, some 90 cm in diameter. (Auforn, 1975).

A witness claims to have seen a crop circle appear. The whirlwind responsible shimmered and then lifted above the crop before wandering away across another field. (Fortean Times no 62 referred to in Wilson 1998, p.147).

In May or June, Jelte Postma was driving in the Sneek area when she heard a buzzing noise, which she likened to a loud wind. She then saw a 1.5m circle spin out very quickly in grass about 20 - 30 cm high. The lay was clockwise, with the grass recovering slightly immediately after being pressed down. The edges were sharply defined and the surrounding grass was completely unaffected. (Randles and Fuller 1993, p. 230).

In an article in the short-lived magazine 'Now', local journalist and UFO author Arthur Shuttlewood described his observation of a circle forming.

One evening there were about 50 of us sky-watching at Starr Hill (also known as Middle Hill) along the Salisbury Road. Suddenly, the grass began to sway before our eyes and laid itself flat in a clockwise spiral, just like opening a lady's fan. A perfect circle was completed in less than half a minute, all the time accompanied by a high-pitched humming sound. It was still there the next day. (referred to in Meaden 1989, Randles and Fuller 1990 p. 103).

During the evening of Saturday 11th July, Ray Barnes, described by Lucy Pringle as a dedicated researcher and observer of nature, witnessed a crop circle form. He was taking his dog for a walk after a thunderstorm earlier that afternoon and it was still raining slightly. Barnes explains:

My attention was drawn to a wave or line coming through the top of the cereal crop. After travelling across the field at an arc, the 'line' dropped to the ground, and radially described a circle in a clockwise direction.

The sketch which Barnes added to his report made clear that the 'line' he describes moved several hundred metres over the field before making the circle, which was about 25 m in diameter. The one end of the line remained still and formed the centre around which the other end drew the circle. Barnes continues:

There are several points to make about the line. It was invisible, just a wave cutting through the corn. In addition, there was absolutely no wind, and the line exhibited no fluid tendencies, that is, its speed was constant and there were no wind waves before or after it. The line just appeared, and there was no disturbance of hedges or trees at the field boundary. The estimated speed of the line was about 80 kph, and there was no visual aberration in front, above or behind it. The line almost disappeared where the ground dips, so it would seem it was maintaining a constant height irrespective of ground contour. The crop heads just 'jiggled', rather than being bent, which would seem to indicate that the line had holes in it like the teeth of a giant comb, or that the line was sufficiently weak for the cereal heads to pop through it when the pressure of them reached a certain level. The circle itself was described radially (not diametrically), and at a constant speed, and was executed in a single sweep. If there were other sweeps, I didn't see them. The peripheral speed of the circle seemed to be about twice that of the line arc speed. The crop circle went down as neatly as if it had been cut by a giant flan cutter. There was absolutely no spring back, which was rather awe inspiring; for if, for instance, you watch a tractor crossing a field there is always some springing back of the flattened crop (Meaden 1991 (2), p.104, Pringle 1999, p.5).

1983 BRATTON ON LITTLETON, WILTSHIRE

One evening late in July or early in August Melvyn, Bell was out riding on the old Ridgeway near Lavington at about eight in the evening, when he became aware of a whirlwind forming a circle in a wheat field below the path. He observed the whirlwind, spinning dust, dirt and other debris upwards only to fall back again, chiefly around the edge of the circle. The 10-12 metre diameter circular flattened area had sharp vertical sides (Meaden 1991 (2), p. 35).

1989 THANET, EAST KENT, ENGLAND

At approximately 12.30 am on 10th August 1989, Wilfred Gomez and a friend were driving along an unclassified road near Lydden on the island of Thanet when they observed a 'solid hurricane of light' with a fuzzy, indistinct top but more clearly defined lower base, hovering over an adjacent cornfield. The column of light was white with a bluish tinge and seemed to be rotating. Mr Gomez wound down his side window and heard a low, even 'humming' sound emanating from the object. The witness observed the column of light for approximately four seconds as they drove past the column, then it 'blinked out to one side', and the humming stopped. The two witnesses drove a short distance up the road before stopping and walking into the field in which the light had been. Because there was a half moon, they soon discovered a 20 m diameter circle with undamaged corn swirled in an anti clockwise direction (Randles and Fuller 1990, p. 105).

On the 13th of November 1989 Terrence Meaden interviewed Mr Sandy Reid, of Dundee, Tayside about an incident that had taken place on the morning of the 27th or the 28th of August. Mr Reid, a naturalist, had for many years studied foxes and their habitats and territories in his Tayside locality. After a calm pleasant night, dawn had broken to reveal a fine morning sky, and Mr Reid was following a trail along the embankment between two fields from where he had a good view into the sloping fields of spring barley which he said was 'still green and turning yellow'. Suddenly his attention was drawn to an unusual noise and a violent rustling in the corn. Thinking perhaps it might be a deer in the barley he froze immediately, but soon realized that it was quite a different sort of commotion talking place a few metres away. He saw how the corn over a circular area was being buffeted by a highly localized movement of air, and that the motion did not progress across the field, but remained fixed to the same area. This continued between half a minute and one minute before the crop quickly went flat over a circular region with a sharp perimeter and with a diameter of 15 to 18 metres. Although the nearest part of the circle was no more than 15 metres distant, he felt no wind himself. He then entered the flattened circle, noticing what he called an 'unusual condition of the atmosphere' and experienced a peculiar sensation in the air. Everything had gone quiet, the noise from the air and the moving corn had stopped and the birds had stopped singing [6]. Reid

1989 DUNDEE, TAYSIDE, SCOTLAND

---

6   In 1999 Charles Mallett experienced a close encounter with a ball of light in a crop circle where he had settled down to spend the night. Just before the light became visible only two metres in front of him, he had "a feeling of being separated from reality" and of finding himself in "an alternative, surreal reality" in which he no longer heard the sounds of nature around him or the traffic from the road below (Brekkestø 2004).

did not recall whether the crop was laid down as a spiral, but when he crossed the circle he noticed that the straws were laid first one way and then the other.

Mr Reid went home to return later with a friend, except this time he approached the field from the opposite direction. In doing so he encountered a second circle some three metres across which he had not spotted earlier. The two circles were 50 metres apart (Meaden 1991 (2), p. 122–123).

1989 HAMBLEDON, SURREY, ENGLAND

On Thursday 17th May at 8 p.m. Vivienne and Gary Tomlinson went for a walk across the fields to Bryony Hill, a local landmark near Hambledon. It was a warm and still evening. When the couple had walked back down from the hill and crossed the first of the two wheat fields, it started blowing. The wind towards Bryony Hill was strong, sending wave after wave of ripples across the crop and making the trees lean over. The Tomlinsons take up the story, as presented by Lucy Pringle:

Suddenly, in a matter of seconds, a band of mist rolled across and down from the top of the hill. It all happened so quickly. The wind pattern changed, the band of mist seemed to come between two trees at the end of the field; continuing on it appeared to be pushing from two directions and surging forwards. At the centre of the mist the wind gathered force, sending strong waves as it went. A whirlwind seemed to appear at this point. It looked like mist or light fog, and was shimmering.

We could hear the noise of the wind. The whistling grew stronger and the wind intensified and reached a high pitch like a set of pan-pipes, ending on one continuous note. The noise was tremendous. The corn was being pushed down as the spinning air made its way towards us. We both looked up to see if there was a helicopter above. Suddenly, there was a strong gust of wind pushing us from the side and from above. The shimmering air circled around us. It was forcing down hard on our heads. We could hardly stand upright, yet it felt as we were being sucked up at the same time. There was a tremendous pressure from both above and below. We felt tingly all over, like pins and needles from head to foot. Our hair was standing on end. All at once the wind scooped us off the path into the cornfield. We took a great buffeting. It was very frightening. Looking down we saw a circle being formed around us. It only took a couple of seconds. A spiral appeared anti-clockwise and grew outwards from the centre, about two metres in diameter. In the centre of the circle there was a small pyramid of corn, the stalks stacked up against each other. The whirlwind split in two, one part going

Formation at Wayland's Smithy, 27th July 2008 (Photo: Axel Kayser)

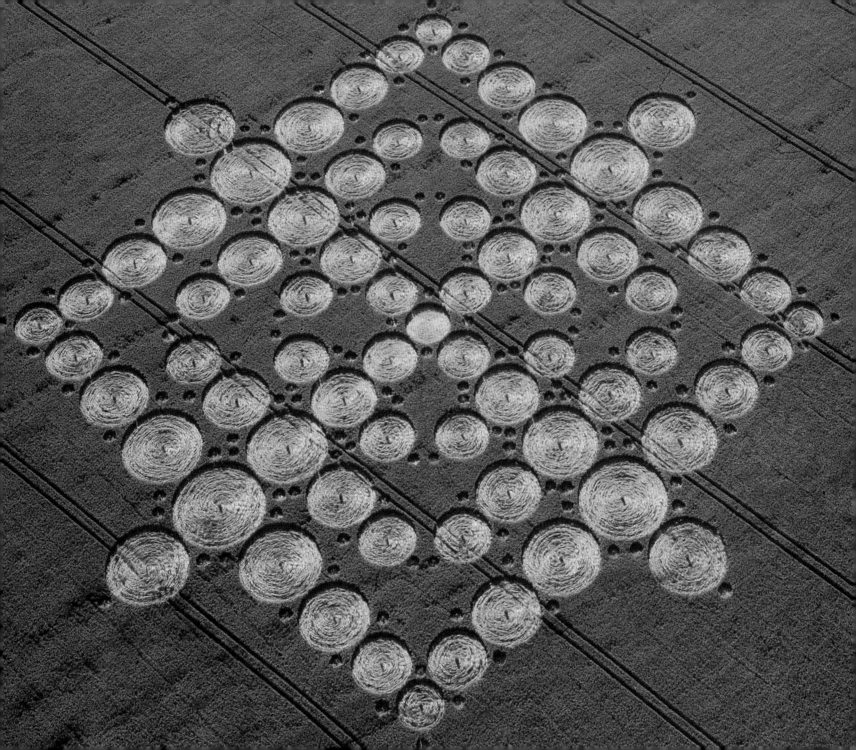

into the distance, skimming over the top of the corn as it went. The second part whizzed past to one side, pushing down the corn and then forming a second circle a little further away. Again, this only took a few seconds. We looked around for the first whirlwind and could still see it, like a shimmering mist, as it zigzagged into the distance. Interesting things were happening in the circle in which we were standing. Miniature whirlwinds were appearing one after the other; small, glistering vortices perhaps four inches apart. They whirled around the corn in small bunches towards the perimeter, gently laying the corn down and enlarging the circle. The wind had dropped completely and it seemed strange watching these shimmering whirlwinds as they spun around. We both turned towards the second whirlwind, which looked like a transparent glowing tube stretching endlessly into the sky. The light was beginning to fade. By now, the miniature whirlwinds seemed to have lost their misty look, appearing more like watery glass with a quivering line inside. They wobbled slowly, still running along the wall of the circle. There also seemed to be fewer of them. It was growing dark, and slowly we made our way back home in silence, stunned by the event. We both felt lethargic and nauseous, and were suffering from shock (Pringle 1999, pp. 1 and 3-5).

1991 WARMINSTER, WILTSHIRE

In 2008 the Ministry of Defence started releasing previously secret files of UFO sightings, which included one report mentioning a crop circle, reproduced as follows on the *This is Wiltshire* website in October of that year:

In July 1991, a driver and his wife pulled off the A350 south of Warminster and watched, spellbound, as a bright whirlwind created a crop circle in front of them. The MoD report read: "Four whirlwinds, spiral from centre of circle – bright white. Swishing noise (distant). Moving around each other in a form of a circle and then disappeared" (This is Wiltshire 2008).

1991 KINGSTON, EAST SUSSEX

Andy Thomas has an interesting eye witness account of a whirlwind-type circle forming in his book 'Fields of Mystery', based on a personal interview carried out in 1995.

One warm and calm Sunday afternoon at the beginning of September, college lecturer Martin Sohn-Rethel, his wife and their three children were walking on the downs which overlook Kingston, Swanborough and Iford in East Sussex. As Martin gazed inland across the fields, one of which, 30 yards away, had not yet been harvested, a strange and very strong gust of wind began to blow. Where they stood, the air was still. He watched as this 'wind' appeared to cross the field of standing crop. Suddenly, in no more than five seconds, about thirty yards from the northern edge of the field, a perfect circle, about 12 metres in diameter, simply appeared in the crop as Martin watched, as if a vortex of air had spun the stems down (Thomas 1996, p. 39-40). Although only Martin was looking in the right direction to see the circle forming, all the family confirmed his description of the strong wind (Thomas 1996 pp. 39-40).

In August 2009, I interviewed computer engineer and inventor Winston Keech, whose interest in UFO sightings led him to the crop circle phenomenon. In July 1991 Keech was behind a hedge on the edge of East Field, when he witnessed a pale luminous disk above the crop in the field. As the disk travelled slowly across the field it was the size of a small dinner plate before expanding to approximately 6 m in diameter. It then became stationary, hovering over the crop; the corn beneath shook, rattled and fell naturally, taking only about 3 seconds. Keech remembers: "The formation occurred no more than 15 metres in front of me. It was that close, which is why I was so shocked at the time". The disk then moved away across the field, contracting as it did so. He went to where he had seen the luminous object and found a small circle of approximately 6 m in diameter (author's interview with Winston Keech in 2009 and 2011).

1991 ALTON BARNES, WILTSHIRE, ENGLAND

In April 1991, a young man was riding his bike near Butleigh when he heard a high-pitched humming sound. Looking up he saw a stationary silver bell-shaped craft project a spiralling vortex of aura-like light into a field. The event occurred in broad daylight and was over in a few seconds. Where the spiralling vortex hit the field, it produced a 13 m crop circle (Wingfield 1991).

1991 SOMERSET, ENGLAND

Ed Sherwood is a researcher into paranormal phenomena who has spent many years studying crop circles and anomalous lights and now runs the website 'Crop Circle Answers'. At about 11pm on July 26th 1992, during a group sky watch near Alton Priors in Wiltshire, he witnessed, from a distance of about a third of a mile away, what he described as 'an amber-orange coloured ball plasma, roughly 20-30 feet in diameter, suddenly materialize low above a hedge and a group of trees. Holding a stationary position for approximately a minute and a half, while appearing to sway from side to side, it then, at an estimated angle of forty-five degrees, quickly descended

1992 ALTON PRIORS, WILTSHIRE

into a wheat field near Draycott Fitz Payne', where it created a crop circle consisting of a single circle and ringed circle (Sherwood 2003).

1994 ARAD, ROMANIA

Still picture from film of balls of light circling over the ground near Oliver's Castle while a crop circle forms (Photo: John Wheyleigh)

The Romanian UFO Journal for 1994 has an interesting account of crop circles being formed in that country. On the 20th June at approximately 4 am, in Arad, Romania near the Hungarian border, Traian Crisan, 48 years of age, was checking his sheep, when he saw a huge light approaching over a nearby wheat field, 'like the moon, but much larger'. When the light came as close as 5 metres to him, a sudden blast of wind blew away his hat and cape and knocked him to the ground.

I lay there clinging to a bush in terror. The bright object was completely round, and it emitted a whistling noise. The object remained motionless hovering above the wheat field for two minutes, before taking off straight upwards and disappearing incredibly quickly. I ran to get help. When I returned, we saw that two crop circles had appeared in the wheat. Both circles measured 6 metres in diameter, with an outer ring measuring 4 metres in width. All the corn within the circle was firmly pressed down in an anticlockwise direction, and the crop was interwoven, or plaited.

The other witnesses confirmed that they had seen a strange light over the field, and had heard a whistling noise (Hesemann 1996, p. 57).

1996 OLIVER'S CASTLE, WILTSHIRE

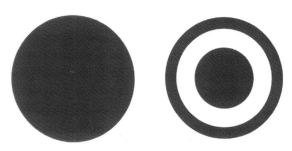

Ed Sherwood's sketch of the crop circle he saw forming in 1992

On the night of 9th August 1996, John Wheyleigh was camping out on the hilltop of Oliver's Castle near Devizes in Wiltshire. In the grey light of dawn he was woken by a strange sound coming from the fields below. Seeing a light in the field, he got out his video camera and filmed the light for a few minutes as it moved around the field. When the light settled in one area of the field, Wheyleigh zoomed in and recorded how the corn went down in what would turn out to be a snow-flake type pattern. The crop circle was completed in four seconds, during which time two balls of light, later joined by two more, circled around. The version of the film which was released to the public only showed the last 7 seconds of footage, the zoomed-in part. However, crop circle researcher Francine Blake and others saw the whole film soon after the event and witness that it lasted for several minutes (Thomas 2002, and Francine Blake, interviewed by the author in July 2005.

On the night of August 9th 1988, a seven sided crop circle surrounded by 173 tiny grapeshot circles appeared next to Tawsmead Copse. Two separate parties appear to have witnessed its creation:

1) Naisha Ahsian and Lili Ruane from Vermont, USA, watching the field from Knap Hill to the north in the very early hours of the morning, saw 'luminosities' spiralling over the field where the formation was found the next morning.

2) Nikki Saville and her brother were watching from Adam's Grave, the barrow which overlooks East Field. While watching the lights they were joined by a couple in their early thirties from a nearby village. They all watched three lights split from the first and moving around the field. The moonlight lit up the ground and allowed them to make out a shape appearing in the field (Thomas 2002, p.71).

On Monday June 7, around 1:30 AM, Robbert van den Broeke woke up, looked outside the window and saw a strange light. He was standing in his bedroom, looking out over the field behind his house. Then he noticed that the light was moving, and actually seemed to be quite close. The colour of the light was a very faint pink, almost white. Suddenly the light stopped about 50 metres from his window and, in just a few seconds, started to expand and transform into an elliptic disc about 10 metres in diameter. Robbert noted how the air around it seemed to tremble, as if it were hot. He then heard a sparkling sound and saw that some kind of electrical discharge seemed to take place under the disc of light. This went on for 8-10 seconds before the light slowly faded and disappeared. Robbert put on some clothes and ran across the garden into the field. At the spot in the field where he had observed the light phenomenon, he discovered a circle of flattened wheat 3-4 metres across. He saw vapour rising from the circle, and bending down to touch the flattened crop, he noted that the plants felt quite warm. Next morning, he discovered a smaller circle of flattened wheat (about 70 cm across) which had appeared adjacent to the larger one. Before he went to bed at 10 p.m. the evening before, he had looked out into the field from his bedroom window and had not seen any circles in the field (Janssen and Ossebaard 2001).

In August 2001, American crop circle researcher Nancy Talbott visited the Van den Broeke household in Hoeven, in southern Holland. The son of the house, Robbert,

1998 ALTON PRIORS, WILTSHIRE, ENGLAND

1999 HOEVEN, THE NETHERLANDS

2001 HOEVEN, THE NETHERLANDS

Top: Andreas Müller's photomontage of the pillar of light which Robbert and Nancy saw outside the window of Robbert's house in Hoeven (Copyright: BLT Research)

Over: The circle in the beanfield as seen the next day from the bedroom window (Copyright: BLT Research)

had for many years been the focus of mysterious events involving unusual light phenomena, crop circles and appearances of strange other-worldly beings. Having visited and interviewed Robbert a number of times, Nancy had got to know him and become a friend of the family.

On the night of the 20th August, Nancy stayed overnight at the Van den Broekes. After the rest of the family had gone to bed at around 11.30pm, Robbert and Nancy remained sitting at the kitchen table chatting about crop circles. They talked till late, and Nancy expressed her frustration that after nearly ten years of intensive study of the phenomenon, she still hadn't got any nearer to understanding how crop circles were made. Before she went up to bed, she said to Robbert, "Crop circles just get more and more of a riddle for me and the whole phenomenon just looks more and more complex the more time I spend trying to understand it! I'm getting a bit fed up with it. Why can't the phenomenon reveal itself to me in a more direct way, and soon?!"

The Van den Broeke family house is right next to a large field, and both the kitchen downstairs and the bedroom at the back where Nancy was sleeping have large windows looking out onto this field, where a crop of beans had been planted that year. At about 3:05am, while Robbert was still in the kitchen downstairs and Nancy had just gone to bed, she heard a few cattle nearby bellowing loudly. With some breaks this went on for about 10 minutes. Nancy was sitting in bed reading and had a direct view through the bedroom window into the field. Then, at about 3:15 am, a brilliant, intense white 'tube' or column of light, about 25 to 30 cm in diameter, flashed down from the sky to the ground. She couldn't see exactly where it was touching down or how close it was. Approximately one second of total darkness elapsed outside and then a second column of the same brilliant white light, slightly edged in a bluish tint, appeared slightly to the left of where the first column had been. Again the room and the outside lit up spectacularly, somehow leaving the intense column of light clearly visible for about one second. Nancy saw that within the column, there seemed to be some kind of spiralling movement. She was half out of bed and in the process of yelling for Robbert when after another second's darkness, a third column of light flashed to the ground. By that time Robbert, who had seen the same thing from the kitchen, was on his way up the stairs to tell Nancy, so he missed the third flash. From the kitchen Robbert had seen that the columns of light had hit the bean-field, just beyond the fence at the back of the garden. Afterwards he reported that the sky had lit up with each tube of light and that the tubes of light were spiralling down to the ground. He had also heard cattle bellowing and noticed a dog next door barking furiously just prior to the appearance of the light-tubes.

By now the rest of the family were on their feet. They had not seen the columns of light, but had been awakened by the shouting. They all went outside. It was a dark night and looking up they could only see the overcast sky. They crossed the garden and headed for the back fence and the farm field. Just over the fence, about five metres into the bean field, barely visible in the light from the house windows, they saw the new crop circle. When they turned a flashlight onto the field they could see that half of the crop in the downed area was laid away from them and the other half was laid toward them. Nancy thought she could faintly see steam rising from the freshly downed beans, which she attributed to the interaction of the tubes of light with night time dew covering the crop.

At dawn the next day, from her bed, Nancy could clearly see the circle in the bean field. Having obtained the farmer's permission, the family entered the field. The circle turned out to be an ellipse of about 12 m by 7 m, with a 6 m long pathway adjoining the northern edge and ending in a crossbar like the capital letter "T". The epicentre of the ellipse was considerably off centre and the northern half of the bean plants, heavy with beans but entirely undamaged, were swirled counter clockwise in what looked to be one wide sweep all the way around the ellipse. The pathway was laid away from the ellipse to its end (BLT Research 2001).

On July 4, 2003 at approximately 7:30 am Central Daylight Time (CDT), retired truck driver Arthur Rantala was up early making coffee in his workshop and watching a weather front that was moving across the Dodge County, Wisconsin area. His workshop was located a few miles from the town of Mayville and the village of Kekoskee, and situated at the top of a hill overlooking a wheat field across the street. Rantala poured his first cup of coffee at 7:35 am, noticing the time on his coffee maker. A few minutes later (at approx. 7:40 am), the rain started falling, the wind picked up, and he noticed that the bark was flying off a hickory tree about 10 feet from his east-facing workshop window. He leaned out of the open window to take a closer look. Rantala then noticed that on the other side of the road, a group of trees "started swinging every which-way." As he followed the trees blowing around, his gaze followed down to the wheat field behind them, where the circles then appeared one by one, right in front of him. The northern-most circle, farthest away from the

Deformed corn stalk from the Wisconsin 2003 crop circle (Copyright: BLT Research)

2003 KEKOSKEE, WISCONSIN, USA

A US Air Force airman inspect the crop circle at Mayville, Wisconsin, July 2003 (Copyright: BLT Research)

road, formed first. Next, the southern-most circle closest to the road formed, followed by the one in the centre. Within roughly 12 seconds, but no more than 15 seconds, all the circles had been flattened. There was nothing unusual in the sky, no lights, no unusual sounds, and no unusual odours.

When a team from BLT Research took samples of the downed corn three weeks later, they found plenty of elongated and exploded nodes. They also found strange changes in some of the heads of corn, in that the stem just below the ear had gone curly, like a pig's tail. These changes were not found in control samples taken from the same field but outside the crop formation. (Read more about BLTs research on pp. 142–147).

However, this was not the end of the story as regards the Wisconsin crop circle. Todd Lemire from the Michigan UFO association visited the site on the 23rd July to investigate, along with Roger Sugden. In the circle he met a Dr. Lietzau and Gary Kahilmer. While they were there, a military helicopter arrived. It circled very low over the formation for a few minutes before flying off again. As the UFO researchers continued to explore the circles, Lemire looked up towards Rantala's workshop on the other side of the road and spotted a man in camouflage uniform watching them through binoculars. This man then got into a car, drove past the field and up to the researchers' cars and noted their registration plates, before returning to the field and walking out to the formation. There he explained that he was in a special US Air Force team tasked with crop circle investigations and that they had inspected two crop circles in Illinois in the previous year, 2002. The airman also stated that he had been on board the helicopter which had circled overhead 45 minutes earlier. Lemire showed him the anomalous features of the corn in the formation and said that they would publish their findings on the Crop Circle News website. The airman said he knew the website. After 10 or 15 minutes in the circle, he went back to his car, made a call on his cell phone and drove away (ICCRA 2003).

It has long been obvious that the British military takes a keen interest in crop circles, but this was the first time that the same was recorded in another country, with a uniformed airman investigating a formation. Read more about crop circles and the military on page 161.

2003 SZCZECINEK, POLAND

On 11th August 2003, Lech Chacinski witnessed a UFO landing at Szczecinek in northern Poland. This was an 'encounter of the third kind' in which Chacinski met aliens face to face, had telepathic contact with them and lost consciousness afterwards. When the UFO had gone, he found a crop circle left behind. The whole remarkable story is told in detail on pp. 97–100 (BLT Research 2003).

2005 RANZANO, FRIULI, ITALY

On 5th June 2005, the newspaper *Il Gazzettino* reported the appearance of a crop circle four days previously near to Ranzano in Friuli, a location which had hosted a crop circle once before in 2003. Caterina Silot, who farms the barley field in question with her husband, was reported as having received 'a sign' that another visitation by 'intelligent alien entities', as she presumed the circle makers to be, was due (Cropfiles 2005). Crop circle researcher Nikola Duper later interviewed Silot and made the following report:

On the 1st June at 10:30 a.m. the woman went to light a candle at the shrine of St Anthony, which is situated at the edge of the field. As she stood there with her back to the field, she was aware of the reflected light of a strong flash behind her. She turned around and saw that a crop circle had formed about 50 metres from the shrine. She didn't think it had been there when she arrived at the shrine. She hurried towards the formation, and as she approached it she saw two balls of light rising quickly towards the sky. They were pinkish in colour, and about 12 cm in diameter (Duper 2005).

2006 HOEVEN, HOLLAND

In October 2006, Nancy Talbott was on another visit to Robbert van den Broekes in Hoeven. Late in the evening of the 19th October, they went together to a field on the outskirts of Hoeven where they had seen and photographed strange light phenomena the evening before. It was a clear, calm evening with a temperature of about 10°C. Talbott takes up the story:

Robbert and I were becoming a little chilled and had begun to walk back along the pathway toward the car when he grabbed my arm and pointed out over the field close to the car, saying " There, there - do you see it?", meanwhile describing a "black cloud" which he could see up over the field. He continued, then describing a "black spiral going down into the ground." I peered into the darkness in the direction he indicated and, at first, saw nothing but the blackness in front of the trees at the end of that field. Then I did see a dark movement of something coming down into the field, just as he said he was certain a new crop circle was at that instant forming.

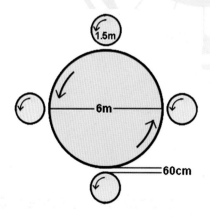

Diagram of crop circle at Hoeven, 2006 (Illustration: Tommy Borms)

Perhaps it is because my eyesight is not as good as his, or because he is more attuned to the crop-circle-making energy than I, but for whatever reason he could see exactly where the new formation was being created. As the spiral descended down into the ground Robbert said that he could feel "something open around his heart" and, then, that he felt as if we were suddenly in the presence of a "higher consciousness," a presence of something perhaps "telepathic," and "very sweet and gentle." We walked down a short earthen ramp into the field and, in 10-15 seconds had reached the new crop circle. I could clearly feel the first small circle when I got to it, because the grass was flatter there and because I got a tingling feeling in my feet. We didn't have a flash-light with us, but did try to take a few photos right away. The new formation consisted of 5 circles, one larger 6 m diameter centre circle and 4 evenly-spaced approximately 1.5 m diameter circles placed around the perimeter of the centre circle. The small circles were placed only 60- 70 cm away from the edge of the larger circle, and all the circles were gently laid anti-clockwise. We stayed inside the formation for perhaps 15-20 minutes, taking photos and discussing the "energy" we felt had been involved this time. Both of us experienced this energy as gentle and soft, somehow more typical of what we would expect in the crop circle phenomenon - and not at all aggressive, as the "tubes of light" had felt when we witnessed the 2001 crop circle occurring in the field behind Robbert's home (BLT Research 2006).

2007 BOSSCHENHOOFD, HOLLAND

The van den Broeke family was again at the centre of some mysterious happenings in June 2007, during which they witnessed the appearance of another crop circle. The account below is based on interviews with Robbert van den Broeke conducted by Nancy Talbott.

The night of the 20th June / 21st June
Before going to bed, Robbert experienced a vision in which he saw a field in the nearby village Bosschenhoofd. He felt what he perceived as "'a strong, sweet and healing 'UFO energy'" over this field. Before going to bed that night, Robbert drew a picture of the crop circle he felt would appear in the field, and left it along with a description of the location observed in his 'vision', so that his father, Peter, could find the field and look for a new crop formation there the next morning. Robbert almost never goes alone into the fields at night anymore, to avoid speculation that he personally has made the crop formations.

Facing page: Crop circle at Walden Hill, Wiltshire, 1st July 2009
(Photo: Eva-Marie Brekkestø)

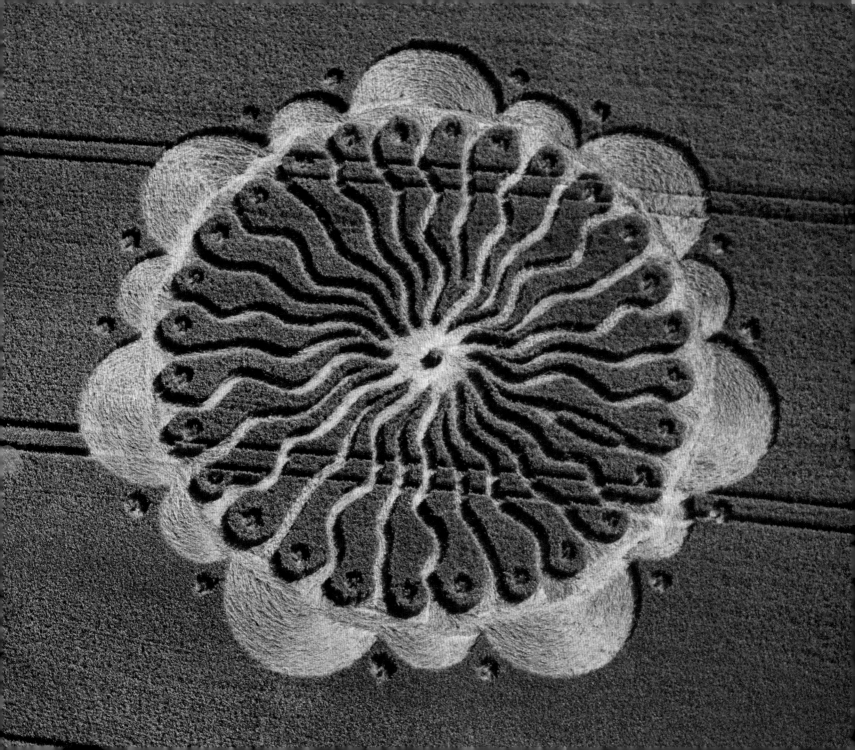

Crop circle in Bosschenhoofd, Holland, 2007, with white powder in the centre (Copyright: BLT Research)

On the morning of June 21st, Peter found Robbert's drawing and at 8 am went to the Bosschenhoofd field, but could not find the crop circle. At about 9:30 a.m. Robbert's mother and a friend, Ellen Gomez, went to the same field and they did find a crop circle, but it did not look exactly as Robbert had predicted. Instead of a 5-circle quintuplet as drawn by Robbert the night before, they found three small circles spaced around the perimeter of a larger one, with a space where the fourth satellite should have been.

June 25th

Robbert had a strong feeling he should return to the field and by 9:30 pm he and Ellen Gomez had arrived and were amazed to find a new circle added to the formation, which now completed the 5-circle design originally seen by Robbert in his 'vision' on June 20th. Robbert observed a smoky 'white mist' floating over the field 80m - 100m away. Robbert walked off towards the mist, and suddenly heard a loud electrostatic crackling noise. He then found a new 4-circle 'thought bubble' with a gentle anti-clockwise spiral in all four circles.

June 27th

In the evening Robbert was again experiencing an intense restlessness and anxiety, which he has learned to recognize usually precedes the appearance of a new crop circle. At about 11:00 pm, his mother and Ellen Gomez accompanied him back to the Bosschenhoofd field, where they first went to see the existing two formations. Robbert began to walk down a tram-line farther into the field. At the distance of about 50m Mrs. v/d Broeke and Ellen could only see Robbert's silhouette. Then both women observed how Robbert's figure suddenly disappeared and that, simultaneously, a small red ball of light appeared over the field 50-75m to the left of where Robbert had been standing a second before. They thought this ball of light was about the size of a golf-ball. For about a minute it moved around just above the crop before it disappeared, and where the ball had just "gone out" Robbert now reappeared. All three of them then walked back to the area of the field where Robbert had originally been standing, and there they found a brand new circle, with a large pile of white powder deposited in its centre. Tests were taken of the powder. It proved to be 99.99% pure magnesium carbonate, which is mostly used as a fire retardant (BLT Research 2008).

WIND AND LIGHT PHENOMENA WHICH SEEM TO HAVE CAUSED THE FORMATION OF CROP CIRCLES

Four children of the Romand family were puzzled when a dog started to bark at 8.30 p.m. on the 27th of September. By their barn was a glowing mass; it was still. One boy threw pebbles and was suddenly knocked to the floor by an 'invisible force'. A luminous red ball was now seen moving away. Next day the police found an oval of grass that was flattened in an anti clockwise swirl and which was sharply delineated. It measured four metres in diameter and had some holes in the centre. A flagpole outside the circle was damaged, with bark torn off the wood, suggesting a considerable force (Michel 1958).

1954 PREMANON, FRANCE

According to the website 'UFOs at Close Sight', the local newspaper Nord-Matin in Lille, France , published on 6th October 1954 an account of a crop circle being formed in a spinach field four days previously. On the night of the 2nd October 1954, a woman and her son heard strange noises outside the house. They both had a look out of the window, to see a red light hovering above a patch of spinach. After a while the light "soared away". The next morning they discovered a circle of flattened, but otherwise undamaged, plants in the spinach patch. A window in the building had also been broken in the course of the visitation ('UFOs at Close Sight').

1954 ST.SOUPLET, NORTHERN FRANCE

At around 2.00 a.m. a man and his wife saw an oval UFO, which they described as looking like a brilliantly illuminated barred window about 9 m long. It hovered stationary for about 45 minutes, projecting lights onto nearby trees and plants. After dawn the circle was found, measuring 8 metres, swirled anti clockwise in the grass beneath where the UFO had hovered. Within the floor pattern were a number of secondary swirls (Randles and Fuller 1990, p. 160).

1969 IBIUNA, BRAZIL

In May 1969 a local newspaper in Ontario featured an incident reported from Chapeau in Quebec province. On 11th May , Leo-Paul Chaput, his wife and children were sitting in the kitchen at the back of their house at Chapeau, when they saw a big white light that lit up the field. The next day three large circles of singed or matted grass were found in the field. Two were circles with rings around them, measuring 10 metres and 8 metres respectively, with 1 metre wide rings. There was also a smaller circle 3 metres wide (The Daily Star, Sudbury 1969).

1969 CHAPEAU, QUEBEC, CANADA

1971 LYNCHFORD, TASMANIA

Mr C. Archer was woken up at 2 a.m. on 25th May by his dogs yelping and barking. A strange humming noise 'like a big, loud generator' was heard. He looked outside but saw nothing. Then the noise ceased. The next day on waste ground an elliptical area of grass and blackberries measuring some nine by five metres was found flattened. In the centre was a 'spiral pattern'. The land had last been seen on the 24th, when it was undamaged. On the 27th the family's healthy four month old kitten died. The police even performed an autopsy, as its presence outside during the event suggested a possible cause. No cause of death was found (Randles and Fuller 1990, p. 161).

1972 RACINE, QUEBEC, CANADA

A married couple saw a UFO resting on the ground about 60 metres from them, and three beings working next to the craft. One of the witnesses rushed towards them. However they boarded the saucer and took off, leaving a circle in the grass about 8 metres wide, with a central standing tuft of 0.70 m diameter (UFOROM database).

1972 WELLINGTON, NEW ZEALAND

The Wellington Times of 6th October 1972 reported that on the night of 1st October, Henry Thomas and his family heard a strange noise. The next day they found a field of grass flattened into a circle of about nine metres diameter (Randles and Fuller 1990, p. 161).

1974 HIGH POINT, NORTH CAROLINA, USA

At 10 p.m. on the 23rd of March, two men were driving down May Road toward Highway 109 when they saw a triangle of pink lights. While descending towards a field it became more red. Next morning they returned to the site and found three circles in the grass. The central one had a diameter of about three metres. The two smaller satellites were a few metres to either side and a little less noticeable (Randles and Fuller 1990, p. 162).

1977 SALTO, URUGUAY

At 4 a.m. on February 18th, rancher Angle Maria Tonna, his family and farmhands were herding cows when the generator-powered lights failed and they saw a 'Saturn-like mass which glowed orange' and was lighting up the barn. The cows were running wild and farm dogs barking furiously as the orange mass rocked from side to side generating a wind strong enough to tear branches off neighbouring trees. The dog Topo flew towards the hovering mass to attack, but froze in his tracks and began to howl when within five metres. Six beams of 'white lightning' streaked from the underside into the ground, and Tonna was struck by a wave of heat and electrical tingles strong enough to paralyze him. The glow now turned red and shot away. At the site where the trees were broken there was a circle 10 metres in diameter flattened and singed into the grass. Three days later Topo was found dead at the exact spot where the glow had hovered. An autopsy by the local vet found that the animal had been 'cooked' by internal heating (Randles and Fuller 1990, p. 163).

John Lewis sent in the following report to "The Unexplained" magazine in 1983:

I live on a ridge 450 feet (135 metres) above sea level, about 100 feet (30 metres) above the adjacent land; it is quite steep in parts on the north side and stretches for about 1 miles (2.5 kilometres). One day, at about noon, I was inside my cottage when suddenly I heard a very loud roaring sound, not unlike an express train. I ran outside to see what it was, but saw nothing; the noise was something like the sound of a falling bomb. I thought no more of this until the following morning when taking my dog for a walk. Then I saw two large circles, about 25 feet (7.6 metres) in diameter, of flattened barley in a nearby field. A neighbour who lives on the north side of the ridge had also heard the roaring noise but could find no cause for it. I wondered if we had heard some part of an aircraft or satellite, or even a small meteor, coming down and, with the local farmer, we investigated the circles, but found no debris at all, just flattened barley. The farmer said that sometimes growing conditions made barley collapse at its base, though he could not understand the almost perfect circle (Randles and Fuller 1990, p.112).

1981 ROSS-ON-WYE, HEREFORDSHIRE, ENGLAND

The Journal of Meteorology for 1990 published a report of a 1988 incident:

1988 NORTON BAVANT, WILTSHIRE, ENGLAND

Mr Sharp of Norton Bavant, Wiltshire heard a sudden noise that he compared to a 'whirlwind' striking his garage not long after dawn one morning in July 1988. Less than 200 metres away, later that same morning, he discovered two newly formed circles. (Randles and Fuller 1990, p. 113).

Mary Freeman was leaving the Avebury stone circle just after 11 pm on July 13th 1988 when she observed a 'large golden disc' which then projected a 'bright white, parallel beam of light' at a '65 degree angle, across the sky towards Silbury Hill'. At the same time objects flew off her car's dashboard, as if invisible energy had swept past.

The next night a quintuplet of five circles appeared in the field adjacent to Silbury Hill, where Freeman had seen the light display the previous night (Andrews and Delgado 1989).

1988 WOOLASTON, GLOUCESTERHIRE, ENGLAND

One evening in July, Tom Gwinnett, a farmer from Woolaston, Gloucesterhire, was driving past a wheat field, when his car's electrics suddenly failed. He was trying to rectify the problem, without success, when he became aware of a strange whirring noise. He looked into the adjacent field, where he saw a dull red ball the size of a football. It was not a solid sphere; rather, it appeared to consist of a cluster of red sparks, and the sparks seem to be coming from the tops of the wheat. Spellbound, Gwinett watched the mysterious ball for a minute or two, the mechanical sound continuing throughout. The object then suddenly disappeared and all was quiet. At that precise moment, the electrical fault on his car righted itself, his headlights came back on and he was able to continue his journey. He didn't inspect the field that evening, but the following morning he discovered a six-metre crop circle at the spot where he'd seen the mysterious ball of red sparks (Meaden 1991 (2)).

1988 AVEBURY TRUSLOE, WILTSHIRE, ENGLAND

At 7.15 a.m. on the 16th of June, Roy Lucas was on a tractor cutting grass verges on the road 3km to the west of the village of Avebury Trusloe when he suddenly noticed, at a distance of 80 metres, what he took to be a puff of white bonfire smoke 5 metres in height. The outer part of this 'smoke' was scarcely rotating, but the middle part which was too thick to see through was spinning rapidly. In a couple of seconds the spinning central column had gone and a residual cloud of fog drifted gently towards the south-west and dissolved after several yards. Five minutes later there was a repeat performance, this time beyond the field boundary. A few hours later the farm manager discovered two single circles (10 m and 9 m in diameter) in a barley field 350 metres west of the location where Lucas saw the first column (Randles and Fuller 1990, p. 106).

1989 PUCKLECHURCH, AVON, ENGLAND

The following is Jacqui Griffiths' own account of her experiences on the 5th of August 1989 as she was driving out of Pucklechurch on the B4465 towards Mangotsfield:

I was passing the Remand Centre entrance and approaching Dennisworth Farm on my right, when I noticed what appeared to be a whirlwind in the field on my right.
I pulled over to stop and watch. The whirlwind was in the field and appeared to

be as tall as the trees which bordered the farm grounds; these trees were rushing to and fro as if in a gale. I could see tufts of grass, twigs and bits of straw whirling round (this is what first attracted my attention).

The whirlwind appeared to move towards and then over the hedge, where it appeared to 'lose' its bottom part, came over the road and then died. It was a very hot and windless day.

The next day a local researcher, Peter Rendall, went to the location of the incident with the witness and discovered several swirled patches of flattened grass and straw close to where the whirlwind was seen. One of the patches was a roughly elliptical area of swirled flattened grass with two spiral centres (Randles and Fuller 1990, pp. 108-109).

On June 28th, soon after midnight, the occupier of the roadside cottage by the path which leads to West Kennett Long Barrow noticed a large ball of light 400 metres distant in a wheat field to the west. At the time of the observation he was walking from the house to the garage, and had a clear view to the illuminated part of the field through a gap in the hedge which borders his garden. He described the ball as orange in colour, adding that it was brighter around the periphery, and he guessed the diameter as 30-40 ft (10-13 m). When first seen, the ball was already low over the field and still descending. The witness watched the base of the ball 'go flat' as it made contact with the crop and/or the ground. The ball then gave 'a little bounce' and after a further 'seven or eight seconds' disappeared. Next morning on leaving the house the witness could see via the gap in the hedge a large circle at the place which corresponded to the position of the light source the previous night, and some smaller circles were evident as well (Meaden 1991 (1)).

1989 WEST KENNET, WILTSHIRE

In the summer of 1990, Richard Flaherty, an experienced wildlife photographer, spent three weeks camping on the downs in the Avebury area. On the 25th of July at 2.30 a.m., he was walking along a track between Windmill Hill and the A4 in the starlit night. He was moving westwards when he saw, in the distance to the south-east, a single column of light coming from high in the sky into a wheat field on the other side of A361 (the road between Avebury and Beckhampton), around 1.25 km away. Because of a ridge he could not see the lower end of the nearly vertical luminous column. He watched the unusual light for six or seven seconds, not fully aware of

1990 WINDMILL HILL, WILTSHIRE

its importance, but nevertheless decided that in the morning he should look to see whether any circles had appeared below. Next morning, both the owner of the field Stephen Horton and Richard Flaherty found that the field contained circles linked by curving paths (Meaden 1991 (2), p. 149).

1991 GWENT, SOUTH WALES

Various UFO sightings have been reported by British police officers to fellow officer Gary Heseltine. The reports are published in the PRUFOS (Police Reporting UFO Sightings) database. This is one of them from June 1991.

In June 1991 two uniformed officers, a police sergeant and a female police constable, were driving in the Blackwood area of Gwent in a rural location when they saw two orange UFOs circling above a farmer's field. They stopped the vehicle and got out to watch. After about 10 minutes the objects disappeared in different directions. As the sun came up, they saw a newly made crop circle under where the objects had been seen darting about the sky. Fearful of ridicule, neither officer reported the incident. They made a pact not to report the incident (Gary Heseltine, PRUFOS).

1993 SALA, NORTH-WEST OF STOCKHOLM, SWEDEN

Crop circle at Sala, Sweden, 1993 (Photo: Clas Svahn)

The time was 5 o'clock in the morning on July 6th 1993 when two brothers in Sala discovered a pair of circles beneath a high-voltage transmission line. One of the brothers told UFO Sweden that he had seen the sky changing colour and felt static electricity in the air early in the morning as he was out walking his dog. Later the other brother went to the place out of curiosity and discovered two swirled circles in a rye field. After a lengthy discussion the younger brother decided to call UFO Sweden anonymously. Their local representative Mats Nilsson investigated thoroughly the same evening and found that the two circles (6 and 12 metres in diameter) had no traces of clay in them, though the surrounding ground was very muddy. Neither could the investigators from UFO Sweden find any tracks leading to the circles from the edge of the field. Both circles were swirled clockwise and Nilsson described their interior as "as smooth as a ballroom floor" (Svahn 1998, p. 249).

1997 TRØGSTAD, NORWAY

In 2005, the Norwegian Crop Circle Group received this report from Jan Olav Mjøs, 35, from Bergen, about an event which took place in 1997:

From 1995 to 2000 I lived at Skjønhaug in the community of Trøgstad in the county of Østfold, Norway. During this period I worked at the local radio station (Radio 5, Trøgstad). Late in the evening on a Friday in August 1997, a few weeks prior to the harvest, I witnessed a crop circle form. Radio Trøgstad has its studio in the same building as the community offices, the police station and the fire station. Between this building and the nearest farm houses, there is a little valley. The slope on the other side of this valley is easily seen from the windows in the building. I was sitting in my office working with the programme plan for the next week, when I looked out of the window and saw a ball of light. It moved in a semi-circle over the farm buildings and then in a vibrating manner above the plants in the field. The distance from the building where I was sitting to this field was perhaps 200 metres, and I would guess that the ball of light was about 2 metres in diameter, although I have to admit that it is difficult to estimate the size of a light object in the dark. The next morning I saw that there was a crop pattern in the field, consisting of a series of seven circles of different sizes. I didn't consider it anything sensational as I knew that crop circles happen around the world, so I took no photographs, but I regarded it as an amusing incident. The whole thing was about 10m by 50m.

Mjøs' drawing of the crop formation he discovered after seeing lights circling over the field in Trøgstad i 1997

Just after midnight on July 22nd 2000, Jerzy Szpulecki witnessed a large UFO landing in a field and leaving a crop formation behind it. During the incident, the power went off in the whole area and car batteries were discharged. Read the whole dramatic story on pp.96–98.

CROP CIRCLES KNOWN TO HAVE FORMED IN A SHORT SPACE OF TIME

In a number of cases people have been in the right place and at the right time to witness that a crop circle must have formed within a certain time frame. So even if these people didn't actually see the crop circle appear, they could confirm that it was formed within a matter of minutes.

Graham Taylor pilots a small four-seater plane, taking tourists out on sight-seeing trips from a small airfield a few kilometres southeast of Stonehenge. His route naturally takes him right over the famous ancient monument. Coming in to land on 7th July 1996, Taylor passed Stonehenge and flew over the field on the other side of

2000 WYLATOWO, CENTRAL POLAND

Diagram of the spiral fractal which appeared at Stonehenge on 7th July 1996

1996 STONEHENGE, WILTSHIRE, ENGLAND

Diagram of the crop circle by the Ridgeway, May 2004

the A303 main road at 17:15, neither he nor his passenger, an American doctor, noticing anything strange.

By 18:00, Taylor was in the air again, this time with an English married couple in the passenger seats.

He was speechless when he reached the same field and caught sight of a fantastic crop circle where 45 minutes before there had been nothing. The strikingly beautiful pattern was a spiral fractal 250 m long consisting of 151 circles (Silva 2002, page XI). Meanwhile the American doctor was driving back towards Stonehenge and was rather taken aback to find himself in a traffic jam as he approached the A303. When he finally got out on to the main road, he saw that there were cars parked all along the verges and that people were already making their way into the field towards the huge crop formation. Several of the security guards at Stonehenge later confirmed to Colin Andrews that there was nothing in the field at 17.15 (Silva 2002, page XI).

2000 WOODBOROUGH HILL, ALTON PRIORS, WILTSHIRE

In July 2008 I interviewed pilot Tony Hughes, who runs the Wiltshire Microlight Centre at Yatesbury. I asked him whether when he was out flying he had ever seen a crop circle which must have been formed in a short space of time. He answered:

On the 19th July 2000 I was flying a crop circle researcher to Everleigh Ashes to photograph a crop circle which had been discovered that morning. From Yatesbury airfield we flew south-east all the way. At half past ten, we passed over Woodborough Hill on our way to Everleigh Ashes, which is about 6 km south-east of the village of Pewsey. On the way back to the airfield at Yatesbury, we followed the same route northwest and again passed over the area near Woodborough Hill a quarter to eleven. Southwest of Woodborough Hill, near Picked Hill, a crop circle had now appeared. Not a specially large or complex one, but still, it's highly unlikely that someone could have made it in 15 minutes. As we flew over the new circle, we didn't see any people on their way out of the field either (author's interview with Tony Hughes 25th July 2008).

2004 THE RIDGEWAY NEAR AVEBURY, WILTSHIRE

On the 30th May 2004, the first major formation of the English crop circle season appeared, and it was discovered in a way which localised its time of formation to within 40 minutes. Microlight pilot J. Melville was flying a passenger to the Stone Avenue next to Avebury Henge. In the absence of anything else to look at, his passenger was going to photograph a so-called 'ghost circle' from the previous season, which was visible between the Stone Avenue and the Ridgeway. As they were overhead the Ridgeway at 11:20 a.m. Melville could confirm that at that time there were no new circles in the neighbouring fields. At about 12 noon, he returned to the same location with a new passenger. There in the young winter barley beneath them was a brand new formation, with an elegant set of 3 spirals inside a simple circle, less than 200m from the ghost circle Melville had been circling over 40 minutes earlier (Anderhub and Müller 2005, pp. 23-25).

2004 WEST OVERTON, WILTSHIRE

On 29th July 2004, a group of Swiss crop circle enthusiasts had booked a series of short helicopter flights with Fast Helicopters Ltd. over the Wiltshire crop circle country. From 11:00 a.m. a temporary landing place was established at Knap Hill, Wiltshire. The helicopter took 3 passengers from the group on each round trip, with the destination alternating between Avebury via Lockeridge and Pewsey via Alton Barnes. At the same time, Guro Parvanova and Irene Lian were on Knap Hill, being interviewed by Stuart Dike about a series of light phenomena they had observed from the same hill a few days previously. Every fifteen minutes they were interrupted by the noise and disturbance of the helicopter landing and taking off again with new passengers. But on one of these occasions, just before 13:30, the disembarking passengers were very excited. On the way to Avebury they had flown over a new crop formation in the form of a snake near to West Overton, about 3 km north of Knap Hill. One of the passengers, Jean-Claude Viret, photographed the formation at 13:18. The passengers told Parvanova and Lian that the pilot was very surprised when he saw the formation as it had not been there on his previous trip to Avebury only half an hour earlier. The passengers on that trip confirmed that the new crop formation must have appeared after they had flown over the area. The leader of the Swiss group explained that on the day before they had been in Glastonbury, where they had meditated on the symbols of the dragon and the snake. Parvanova and Lian headed off immediately to find the formation and by 14:00 they were on site and had confirmed the location. Parvanova then contacted me and told me the whole story. Already the next morning the farmer destroyed the formation (author's conversation with Guro Parvanova 29th July 2004.

The laid corn stalks in the snake formation at West Overton, July 2004, were arranged in a braid (Photo: Eva-Marie Brekkestø)

2005 WADEN HILL, WILTSHIRE

The American artist and crop circle enthusiast Rod Bearcloud Berry has spent many summers in Wiltshire exploring crop circles. On the 16th July 2005, he had a special experience on Waden Hill, a stone's throw from Avebury Henge. He published the story from which the following extract is taken on the Crop Circle Connector website:

Bearcloud's photo of the sunrise from the crop circle at Waden Hill in 2005 (Photo: Rod Bearcloud Berry)

I woke up the next morning early at around 2:50 a.m. I got dressed feeling that the first place I wanted to go to was Avebury. At around 3:20 am I arrived at the field near the Red Lion Inn [Bearcloud means the field north of Waden Hill, facing the southern embankments of Avebury Henge where the road makes a sharp bend -Ed.]. I pulled off the road and examined the field in the dark. I had an advantage because I had a set of high powered Night Hawk optical night vision binoculars. I didn't see anything in the field however, even though I could see it reasonably well. The tramlines were visible on the lower end of the field in the binoculars and the hill top was silhouetted against a black sky. I got back into my car and began to drive off. In that moment, I felt I wasn't satisfied with my survey. I backed up my car a few feet and got out again and reassessed the field. I still saw nothing. I drove from there to East Field where I waited for the light to arrive for the morning. Then at about 4:15 am or so, it seemed light enough out to see the fields. I decided to drive back to Avebury as I kept feeling something and wanted to have a look in brighter light. I arrived at about 4:45 a.m. back at the field near the Red Lion Inn. There, clearly visible on the side of the hill was a new formation. I stood in shock, as I knew the formation had not been there at 3:30 a.m. I made my way down the tramlines and walked into a beautiful pristine Star glyph [Bearcloud's name for crop circles - Ed.]. I found no evidence along the way that led me to believe anyone else had been there earlier than myself. In the hour that I was there it didn't seem as though anyone else had spotted it yet, as no one arrived while I was there. I could tell immediately that it was related to the circle and the triangle. In the outer perimeter of the formation were some square spiral shapes. There appeared to be twenty four of them in the band. I looked out towards the light on the horizon and just as I did the sun's first rays peeked over the horizon with golden orange glow. What a great start to a beautiful morning.

Facing page: the crop circle which Bearcloud discovered on Waden Hill, July 2005 (Retouched photo: Steve Alexander)

The same day at 9:30 a.m. the farmer, Mr Farthing, drove into the formation with his combine harvester and damaged it severely. Unfortunately no photos were taken

of it in its pristine state, but Steve Alexander was able to retouch a photograph he got of the partly destroyed circle to show how it would have looked (see photo on the previous page) (Crop Circle Connector 2005).

2007 KNAP HILL BY ALTON PRIORS, WILTSHIRE

Computer engineer and inventor Winston Keech has spent countless nights out on the hills hoping to film light phenomena and, if possible, a crop circle forming. At about 11 pm on the 6th July 2007, on the top of Knap Hill, he rigged up his various still and video cameras, among them a light sensitive VX2100 film camera and an image enhancing film camera connected to a JVC D-700 recorder. London paralegal and private investigator Gary King has also spent many nights on the hills of Wiltshire. That night he also got a hunch to do at night watch at Knap Hill. He and his partner Paula Presdee-Jones arrived there at about 01.30 a.m.; it was now the 7th of July. He recognized Keech, whom he had met for the first time at the Silent Circle crop circle cafe, some hours earlier, where they had exchanged a few sentences without mentioning their plans for the night. Keech showed them the cameras, all set up on tripods. It was at that time too dark to see the fields below them with the naked eye. At about 01.35 am Keech made a sweep with the image enhancing camera, and in the viewfinder of this camera they could clearly see that there was no crop formation in the vast East Field below them.

Keech's plan was to do a sweep like this about every half hour. But the three crop-watchers got into such an interesting conversation that they totally lost track of time. At 3.13 a.m. however, the conversation came to an abrupt halt when a powerful flash of light lit up the whole valley. The flash, which was like a lightning flash, was registered by the light sensitive cameras as electromagnetic noise lasting just four thousandths of a second. Keech now realised that the four hour long tape on the video cassette must be about to run out. Later it turned out that it had in fact finished just two seconds after the flash. During the night the cameras had filmed lights from houses and villages in the neighbourhood as well as the lights from passing cars on the other side of East Field. They would also have registered the least activity with lights such as torches or laser measuring devices if these would have been used in the fields under Knap Hill. King had a feeling that the flash of light must have had some connection with something happening in East Field. The time was now 3:20 a.m., and Keech did a quick sweep with the most sensitive camera. In the viewfinder they could now see that there was a shadow in the field. Impatiently the three sat

Facing page: East Field with the huge new formation photographed from Knap at 03:51 on the 7th July 2007 (Photo: Winston Keech)

and stared out at the dark field waiting for it to be light enough to discern any details. Finally at 03:45 it was light enough for them to vaguely make out the formation in East Field. At about four o'clock they could clearly see the scale of the huge crop circle in the middle of the field. King and Presdee-Jones decided to drive to the southern end of the field to enter the crop circle from there. Keech stayed upon Knap Hill and filmed the others as they entered the enormous formation. The pattern was about 350 m long by 60 m wide, containing over 150 circles and flattening over 20,000 square metres of corn (author's interview with Gary King 7.7.2007, sequence of events in this account confirmed by Winston Keech).

2008 KNAP HILL NEAR ALTON PRIORS, WILTSHIRE

On the night of the 26th/27th July 2008, there appeared the second of four formations to be found that season in East Field. A number of people were out and about in the area that night, among them Karen Bishop, who was interviewed the next day (27th July) by Juliane Gibsone. She reported:

I was here last night at East Field. There were many of us watching as well. And then about three o'clock this morning people observed orbs, - over towards where The Swallows are. And then those travelled over towards this field here (pointing at East Field), the East Field. Half past four this morning, nothing. Half past six, there she was, absolutely wonderful. My husband and I were the first in. There was no one here at that time, that was half past six. About sevenish two others turned up who were spending the evening at The Swallows. So there were four of us about seven o'clock this morning and then nothing until about nine. But I'm told that about three o'clock this morning there were orbs. [What Karen refers to as 'orbs' are more usually called 'balls of light'.] The light show seen coming over from The Swallows and coming over into the field (pointing at East Field). A third lady came through just shortly afterwards, I think she was Australian, and she herself had left Adam's Grave at about half past four, walked through the field, seen nothing what so ever, up to The Swallows. And then, while she was in the Swallows, she observed the new formation and came down to join us. (Julian Gibsone 2008).

The crop circle which appeared on the 7th July 2007 at East Field
(Photo: Eva-Marie Brekkestø)

CONTRADICTORY EYE WITNESS REPORTS?

Eye witness accounts can sometimes appear confusing and contradictory. How can
it be that some people see crop circles being made by whirlwinds, while others hear
strange sounds? Some people see balls of light to which they attribute some sort of
conscious awareness, while others see physical craft and extra terrestrial beings
making crop circles. Perhaps crop circles come from a number of different sources.
Do the universe, extra-terrestrials, our planet and our own subconscious minds all
create crop circles?

Or might it all fit together in another way? Does the phenomenon take different
forms according to what people 'need' to see in order for their interest to be spurred?
Or is it that we ourselves are part of the creative process, affecting the phenomenon
with our preconceptions about how existence and the universe works? We'll return
to this discussion on pp. 173–183 in the section *An interactive phenomenon.*

CHAPTER 4

LIGHT PHENOMENA, UFOS, WHIRLWINDS AND PLASMA

LIGHT PHENOMENA

When today's crop circle enthusiasts talk to Wiltshire locals about the strange lights and shining objects they have seen in the area, the reply is often that such light phenomena have always been observed here. Certainly ever since the systematic reporting of crop circles began in England in the 1980s, mysterious lights have also been reported alongside the crop circles.

In this chapter we're going to look at a number of incidents where such lights have been observed. In some cases people have reported seeing lights in places where a crop circle would subsequently be found. In other cases, lights have been seen in crop circles that have already formed, or in areas where crop circles often appear. Many of these lights have also been photographed and filmed.

Mysterious lights in the night sky have generally been classified as UFOs, while lights closer to the ground have variously been described as beams, columns, tubes and discs of light, sometimes glowing red and other times shining white; but the shape which has most commonly been reported in recent times is the 'ball' of light. These have become such a feature of crop watching that 'ball of light' has become a standard phrase in crop circle parlance, often abbreviated to BOL. They seem to be the size of a football or basketball but also to vary quite a lot. Balls of light are often

Facing page: Crop circle at Cherhill, July 2008 (Photo: Axel Kayser)

pure white but on other occasions have glowed yellow or orange. They can also change size in the course of an observation. Even more strangely, films have shown balls of light maintaining a constant apparent size irrespective of their distance from the camera.

We will also examine the case of Hessdalen in Norway, where strange light phenomena have been regularly observed for many decades past. Occasions on which light phenomena have been observed at the same time as crop circles have formed are discussed in chapter 3.

'BALLS OF LIGHT' CAUGHT ON CAMERA

Balls of light are quite often seen in the Wiltshire crop circle country, but they are hard to capture on camera as they move fast and appear and disappear without warning. Several people have managed to get some video footage, nevertheless. In 1991 Steve Alexander stood on Milk Hill and filmed a ball of light moving over the fields at Stanton St. Bernard. Donald Fletcher was filming a crop circle from the hilltop at Barbury Castle in 1999 when his camera caught a ball of light moving through the crop circle before setting off at great speed across the countryside. Bert Janssen in 2000 filmed a ball of light moving through a crop circle at Martinsell Hill. Andy Buckley in July 2000 filmed several balls of light moving out of a field with a crop circles in it and around Woodborough Hill. In 2005 he also filmed a ball of light in the sky, which shone steadily for about 20 seconds before fading and then disappearing. In May 2009, Roy Leraand was in the air over a crop circle at Peaks Down, Oxfordshire when he filmed a ball of light moving over the field below. In June 2009, the Norwegians Thomas Peterson and Lars Olaussen filmed a ball of light moving fast over the fields under Golden Ball Hill.

These are just some examples of the many authenticated cases where reputable witnesses have recorded footage of balls of light in association with crop circles. These balls of light seem to have some strange characteristics. Sometimes, as in the instances referred to above, people can see them, take pictures of them and film them. In other cases, however, the lights cannot be seen with the naked eye, but become visible on film and in photographs when these are developed or viewed later. Such was the case with Donald Fletcher's 1999 film. It has also happened that balls of light have been visible to some people present but not others, which is puzzling.

Top: Still picture from Steve Alexander's film from Milk Hill in which a ball of light moves over the fields below (Photo: Steve Alexander)
Centre: Still picture from film of the crop circle at Peaks Down, with a ball of light (bottom right) moving over the fields (Photo: Roy Leraand)
Above: Still picture from film taken from Golden Ball Hill where a ball of light (bottom left) moves over the field below (Photo: Lars Olaussen)

And it's mysterious how they tend to appear and disappear so suddenly. One attempt at an explanation is that the balls of light belong to another reality or dimension from ours. They seem to move in and out of our reality, perhaps becoming visible to us when we are somehow susceptible to different dimensions of reality from those we normally perceive. Maybe the crop circle locations represent places in the landscape where the veil between different realities is thinner than normal?

SOME OBSERVATIONS OF BALLS OF LIGHT

1983 AVEBURY, WILTSHIRE

Around 10 o'clock one evening in November 1983, life-long resident of Avebury, Heather Peak-Garland, left her house on the High Street for a quiet stroll with her dog. As she entered the south-western quadrant of the henge monument at the edge of the village, she observed what she first took to be the full moon. Upon looking closer she realized that this 'moon' was in fact, a soft yellow-white orb of light, gently drifting towards her position from the direction of Beckhampton in the south-west. The luminous globe moved in silence over the earthen ditch and bank, before finally settling down just inside the ring of stones. It then blinked out like a light bulb being switched off (Deveraux 1999).

1999 MILK HILL, ENGLAND

Charles Mallett has been studying the crop circle phenomenon intensively for over 15 years and has spent many nights in crop circles. He has often seen strange lights over the fields, but his most spectacular sighting occurred in 1999, when he had a very close encounter with an orange ball of light. I interviewed Mallett in 2003 and afterwards he kindly contributed the following account for my website, complete with the drawing reproduced opposite:

On May 2nd 1999 a new formation was discovered in a field of oilseed rape at Milk Hill, Wiltshire. Visiting the glyph on the day of its discovery and carefully examining it left me and my partner in no doubt that it was a genuine event and worthy of additional attention.

On the night of May 3rd 1999, my partner and I, as well as a friend of ours, re-visited a new formation that had been discovered in a field of oilseed rape at

Drawing of Charles Mallett and the ball of light in the Milk Hill corp circle, 1999 (copyright: Charles Mallett)

Top: Ball of light filmed over Huish Hill (Photo: Ed Sherwood)
Middle: Ball of light photographed from a crop circle near
Silbury Hill.
Above: Detail from picture above (Photo: Sten Fredriksen)

Milk Hill the day before. I planned to spend the night in the circle, while my partner and friend stayed on the hillside overlooking the field. By 22:00 we were in our respective night spots and settled down. It was a clear mild and starry night with virtually no wind. After sitting for an uneventful two hours, something subjectively strange enveloped the circle, or at least the part of it where I was sitting, as if the air pressure and all the environmental conditions had dramatically changed it into a surreal and different place. No longer could I perceive sounds of wildlife or the distant traffic noise that just some moments earlier had been all too objectively present. This felt very odd indeed.

After several minutes an even stranger situation arose. From my position in a circular element of the glyph I suddenly noticed a sphere of light the size of a soccer ball emerge from nowhere and hover just above the ground no more than ten metres from my position. It was partially obscured by a standing tuft of rape-seed plants at the centre of the circle but was nevertheless very obviously there and grabbed my attention completely. The light sphere remained still and didn't do anything or change its form in any way at all, it just hung there, for what seemed a very long time. Time enough for me to move my position slightly to get a better view of the object. There was by this time no doubt at all, for whatever reason this orb of subtle orange and yellowish light had appeared right in front of me in the crop circle. I sat in a passive state for the time it remained in view, rather spellbound. Throughout the whole event the atmosphere seemed highly charged and extremely bizarre. After a further short period of time the light faded out slowly and disappeared. Some moments later the atmosphere returned to "normal". I then realised that all the external environmental sounds and stimulus were also back. At this point I fell right off to sleep, very odd in itself after such an odd experience, and woke the following morning wondering if it had happened at all, then I remembered that my watchers on the hill were also in situ and decided to wait for them to collect me as arranged and see what they had to say.

They arrived and immediately started blurting out how they had seen an orange light streaking across the field at about midnight towards the formation. They said that as it reached the edge of the glyph it disappeared from their view and they did not see it again. When I told them of the encounter I had had they were stunned and felt sure that what they had seen tied in with what was going on down in the circle just 600 meters away. (Charles Mallett, pers.comm. 2003).

2001 KNAP HILL, WILTSHIRE

For many years past, Ed Sherwood has been observing and photographing various light phenomena, many of which he has publicised on his website Crop Circle Answers in the 'Sightings' section. Sherwood has the ability to know in advance when light phenomena are going to appear, and even to 'see' them before they become visible to the naked eye. On the evening if the 23rd July 2001, he was out on Knap Hill near Alton Barnes. At approximately 9:40pm he witnessed a bright amber-orange coloured luminosity that suddenly appeared low above the crest of a Huish Hill, about a mile east of him. Like a large slowly rising 'fire ball', the luminosity made no discernible noise, remaining visible for about a minute and a half before suddenly 'blinking out' and disappearing against the late dusk sky. The weather conditions at the time were a mostly clear sky, with good visibility, no precipitation, and very little wind. Sherwood also filmed the luminosity with a Sony Handycam set in 'Night Vision' mode.

PHOTOGRAPHS OF BALLS OF LIGHT
1999 SILBURY HILL, ENGLAND

In 1999 I was in England to see the crop circles for the first time. The first formation I visited was the fractal design which appeared on 24th July at West Kennet, within sight of Silbury Hill. Although the circle was already three weeks old when I visited it, it was a big experience for me. I had travelled there with my husband Sten, and we took many pictures of the formation with our first digital camera, which we had bought specially for the trip. Amongst others, Sten took a series of photos facing in a southerly direction of me standing in the formation. Neither of us noticed any strange light phenomena at the time, but on one of the pictures, a few metres above the ground and about four metres to the right of me, there is some kind of luminous object about the size of a basketball. The picture on the left was shown to a professional photographer who assured us that there couldn't be any fault in the memory card, as the light was not visible on the preceding or following pictures in the series. Nor could the light be coming from a source in the background landscape, since it is sharper than the background and must therefore be closer and in the air. And there are no roads or houses within the range of visibility in a southerly direction from that hill either, so there is no question of car lights or reflections from a window being involved. Later, Charles Mallett told me that he and his former partner Francis

Top: Crop circle at East Field, July 2005
(Photo: Eva-Marie Brekkestø)
Centre: Two balls of light can be seen next to each other on the right of the formation at East Field, July 2005 (Photo: Lene Ørntoft)
Above: Two balls of light can just be seen a little to the left of a crop circle on Overton Hill, July 2006 (Photo: Egil Fylling)

had seen many balls of light in that particular crop circle.

2005 EAST FIELD, ENGLAND

In July 2005, Lene Ørnhoft from Norway visited several crop formations in Wiltshire and took lots of photographs. On the afternoon of 31st July, she was up on Knap Hill, where there is a superb view over the countryside below, including over East Field. She took several pictures of the crop circle which had been visible there since 3rd July. Amongst the pictures were two taken in quick succession? The first, taken at 17:19, shows some strange bright dots on the field just by the crop circle. These are not visible on the second picture taken a minute later.

2006 WEST OVERTON, WILTSHIRE

In July 2006, Egil Fylling, also from Norway, visited a number of crop circles in Wiltshire. On 31st July he took several pictures from West Kennet Long Barrow, facing north towards the crop circle on Overton Hill. On one of the pictures, two balls of light can be seen over the fields just by this crop circle.

UFOS

Strictly speaking it would be correct to include the 'balls of light' phenomenon discussed above as a kind of UFO - after all, they fly, and they are unidentified, even if they don't seem to be objects in the normal sense of the word. However, what I refer to in this section on UFOs and crop circles is the 'classic' unidentified flying object: some kind of a craft or vehicle. For many years, accounts have circulated about 'UFO landings' leaving circular marks behind them, often in grass or reeds, and I have already mentioned several such accounts in chapter 3. In this section I will describe three more detailed and recent reports of UFOs in connection with crop circles.

2000 WYLATOWO, POLAND

The following is a résumé of an interview Nancy Talbott made with Jerzy Szpulecki in 2004:

In the early morning of July 22nd, 2000, Jerzy Szpulecki, a farmer in the rural area of Wylatowo, central Poland, was working late at night on a new house he was building on the edge of a wheat field. At 12:15 am, the lights in his house suddenly went out and he came downstairs to check for a short-circuit. As he reached the ground floor he could see, through the large windows in the front of the house, that all of the street-lights on the nearby road were also out, and that there were no lights in the houses nearby. Almost immediately he then saw a "strange red light" in the sky coming down very slowly towards the field in front of his house. The light was a very bright red, spherical in shape, about 20m in diameter. As the light came closer, he saw what looked like a rotating "white fog" above the red light. As this strange object got closer to the ground, it began to enlarge into a much bigger, but still round, object and seemed to "discharge something into the air around it." As the object descended to about 20m above the ground, he began to notice a pressure on his body. And, as it landed, multiple "arms" suddenly extended out of the centre of the object, slowly bending down to the ground. On the ends of each of the "arms" there was a round, violet-coloured light-ball. These balls were so bright they became difficult to watch because it hurt his eyes.

At this point the witness noticed that there were at least three cars stopped on the road next to the field, their occupants apparently also watching the object. The next day he heard from other villagers that "many" people had seen the glowing red ball of light as it crossed the sky.

The object sat touching the ground for about a minute, before the protruding arms retracted and the object rose into the air a few metres and then descended into the field again, a short distance away. Many sparks also accompanied this second landing of the object, but these sparks were coming up to the object from the ground. Finally, after sitting on the ground for about a minute its red glow became so intense that it lit up the room in which the witness was standing.

Szpulecki estimates the amount of time that had elapsed from when he first saw the object to when it disappeared as about 7 minutes. Although when he had first spotted the object he thought it was something on fire, it became clear to him during the sighting that the field did not catch fire.

He states he was profoundly moved and completely awed and amazed by what he had seen, stating that it was beautiful and that he had not felt threatened or been afraid. This intense emotional response lasted for about half-an-hour after the object had departed.

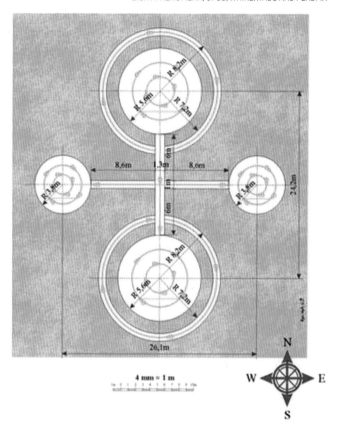

Diagram of crop circle at Wylatowo, drawn by Ewaryst Zylkowski (copyright: BLT Research).

Since the electricity in the house was still out Szpulecki went back upstairs to retrieve his wristwatch before returning to his home and discovered that it had stopped at 12:15 a.m.

The next morning, a neighbour informed Szpulecki that there was a strange marking in the wheat field. It turned out that it was in the precise location where the object had landed the night before. Furthermore, the marking (in the form of a cross with circles at the end of the four arms) was similar to the strange object itself with its arms extended, ending in the smaller violet light spheres on the ends of each arm. The electricity in the area was still not working and many cars had dead batteries. When coming to repair the electric lines, the power company reported that the electricity was out in the entire area, and that they had not been able to figure out the source of the power failure. Over the next week or so it was learned that all the vehicles within about a 500m area around the field had experienced battery failure.

After interviewing Szpulecki, Talbott kept in touch with events in the rural area of Wylatowo.

Two further crop circles were discovered there later the same summer. And in 2001, a crop formation was again found in exactly the same field where Szpulecki had seen the UFO land in 2000. This formation was a good deal more complex in design. Talbott reports that in subsequent summers, crop formations have continued to appear in this area of Poland. Meanwhile, there was to be a final and most bizarre twist to the original Wylatawo crop circle story. On July 6, 2001, in the village of Lublin in south-eastern Poland (about 400 km from Wylatowo), Robert Zmuda was fishing for his dinner and caught a large carp-like fish with a peculiar marking embedded in the skin on both sides of its body. Because Zmuda, a fisherman for many years, had never seen anything like this before, he photographed the carp prior to dispatching it to his dinner table. Later Zmuda happened to see a TV show about the crop circles in Wylatowo, and one of the photographs aired was of the cross-like crop circle found in Wylatowo in 2000. He immediately recognised the design as being essentially the same as the one on his fish!

2003 SZCZECINEK, POLAND

At a conference in Poland in October 2006, crop circle researcher Nancy Talbott met Lech Chacinski, who had been invited to talk about a UFO experience he had had three years earlier. Nancy interviewed him through an interpreter and published a full account of the story on her website, including photographs and drawings supplied by Chacinski. What follows is a shortened version of that account.

At 4:20 am of August 11, 2003, Lech Chacinski, a truck driver who lives in Wierzchowo in Poland, was driving to work. As he approached a bridge near Szczecinek he observed three figures on the road in front of him, the one in front with his hand raised as if in greeting. As he brought his car to a stop, the trio walked toward him and he at first assumed they were men dressed in uniforms similar to astronauts' space-suits. However, as they came closer to the driver's side window he realized there was something disturbingly extraordinary about them. Feeling almost frozen as the humanoid at the apex of the triangular group reached the driver's-side door, Chacinski could see a darkened helmet with a visor of some transparent material, through which he saw two large (3cm diam.) round black eyes, but no other facial details. As the full realization of what he was seeing overcame him, Chacinski wanted to drive away immediately, but a blinding 'beam of light' shot out from a rectangular chamber on the top of the leader's helmet, and Chacinski lost consciousness. When he awakened moments later he felt calm and knew the leader was telling him telepathically that he didn't have to be scared. He heard the question, "Do you hear us?", and mentally responded "Yes," after which he was asked to get out of the vehicle, which he reluctantly did.

Chacinski describes these entities as being about 170 cm tall, with a basically human form (2 arms, 2 legs, a torso and a head), wearing tight-fitting, seamless overalls of a dull silvery, elastic foil material. He states that these overalls seemed to be pumped up from the inside and were integrated with their shoes and mittens. On their heads were helmets with some sort of a band around the forehead which had a light source in the centre, and on the top of the helmet there was something that Chacinski thought was a communication device. He saw no insignia anywhere on their clothing, but on their chests were colourful, blinking, rectangular boards with seven lights in each row, each light a different colour. He cannot remember the combination of colours, but states that the lights were falling down in a sequence one by one, like a fountain. They also had packs on their backs which looked like those worn by astronauts or cosmonauts.

During the approximately 15-minute encounter, Chacinski telepathically perceived multiple questions put to him by these beings, such as: "What material is your vehicle made of?", "How does it work?" and "What kind of fuel does it use?". Chacinski did

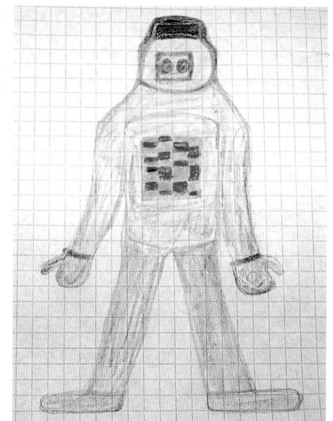

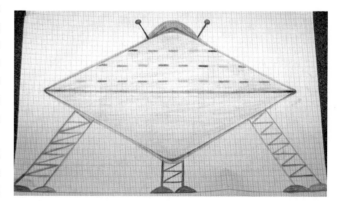

Crop circle at Szczecinek in 2003 (Photo: Rajmund Welnic)
(Copyright: BLT Research)

his best to answer and noted that they expressed surprise upon hearing how his vehicle operated. They also indicated interest in his clothing, in particular his belt and shoes. (This detail is of great interest, in that beings encountered in another Poland contact also showed great interest in that witness's leather belt and shoes.)

The leader, who was the only communicator, then stated that they had come to deliver a message to the inhabitants of Earth, and Chacinski had the impression that he was being charged with the responsibility of spreading this message as widely as possible. In essence the message was that we must care for ourselves and our planet, and that if we continue to disrespect the laws of Nature, the result will be catastrophic.

Why he had this encounter and this message was delivered to him, he has no idea. Chacinski was apparently able to ask only one question of these beings, "Where do you come from?" to which they replied "Eight Galaxy." They also told him they would return, although with no details as to when, where, or for what purpose.

Truly awed by the ongoing encounter, Chacinski next watched as the three beings rose up about 3m into the air and "floated" across the field adjacent to the road to a very solid-looking metal-like disc about 300m away which he had not noticed until this moment. Lech thinks the body of the UFO was about 50m wide by about 20m tall, emphasizing that his drawing ability does not allow for a fully accurate representation of the UFO. There were three rows of individually coloured "windows" across the upper half of the UFO and three sets of 5m long, girder like legs, each set ending in two separate round feet which apparently stabilized the UFO on the uneven ground near the top of the hill. Lech is not absolutely certain that these "feet" were actually touching the ground. On the very top of the UFO were an opaque chamber and two "antennae". The beings landed close to the craft and then walked beneath it, at which point a beam of very bright blue-white light shot out from a round hole which opened up on the underside of the ship. This light "took the three beings up into the UFO" and the hole closed, after which a coloured smoke or fog enveloped the craft. The UFO then floated over the ground for about 50m, stopped briefly during which time the "smoke" dissipated, and then flew away at a 70° angle toward the SE, making a "sssssss" sound.

Once the UFO had departed, an imprint of multiple circles could be seen in the field, in which the plants were swirled and flattened, with smaller circles in the same areas relative to the feet Chacinski saw beneath the craft.

As Chacinski got back into his car after the UFO had departed, a man he knew pulled up next to him, asking if he needed help. Saying that "No," he was OK, Chacinski suddenly realized he had seen no other cars driving by during the entire incident and wondered if the humanoids had somehow caused this. He went on to work, where at first he said nothing about the incident to his colleagues. He did, however, call the police anonymously to report the imprint in the crop and then went home for awhile and told his wife about the experience. They discussed what he should do, in particular regarding the "message" he had received, and Chacinski reports that he did not want to say anything about his morning's encounter. But that afternoon, back at work, he decided to notify the police again, this time identifying himself and describing the entire event. He then also told his colleagues and others, subsequently enduring ridicule and some "very bad times," with many people laughing at him and making fun of his report.

Nancy Talbott also found out that a year or more prior to her interview with Chacinski, her interpreter Less Hodun had met Chacinski at a symposium in Police, Poland and had asked him if he had ever experienced any previous unusual situation. The following is Chacinski's answer as told to Less Hodun:

About two weeks prior to the Szczecinek encounter Chacinski and his wife were watching TV in their home. It was around midnight when Chacinski's attention was drawn toward what looked like a point of light, about 3 cm in diameter, moving horizontally from left to right along the top edge of the wall near the ceiling. Chacinski said nothing, but as he watched the point of light he felt himself becoming mesmerized. All of a sudden the point of light dropped down to the height of his head and flew straight at him, going directly into his left eye. He ran into the bathroom, washed his eyes vigorously with cold water, and then came back into the room. At this point he asked his wife if she had seen anything strange, but she had not (BLT Research 2007).

Top: Mike Booth's own illustration of the objects he saw at Boreham Down (Mike Booth)

Above: Mike at the field, two days after the sighting (Photo: Mike Booth)

2005 BOREHAM DOWN, WILTSHIRE

During the winter of 2005/6, I corresponded with Mike Booth of Marlborough, Wiltshire and in July 2006 Terje Toftenes and I interviewed him on the spot where he had made a remarkable observation the year before. At 18.30 on the 21st June

Crop circle at Boreham Down, June 2005 (Photo: Steve Alexander)

UFO at Marskär, Sweden, caught on camera by Kåre Kårevall in 1956
(Copyright: UFO Sweden)

2005, Mike Booth was cycling along the country road from Marlborough to Alton Barnes, a route he took several times every week. It was a lovely summer's evening, with clear skies and no wind.

Mike Booth continues:

At Boreham Down, coming down the hill from Lockeridge, my attention was caught by three white, metallic objects in the field above the road [the land slopes up here from the road towards West Woods - ed.]. I immediately stopped and very quickly realized that I was looking at something that I had never seen before. The objects were white, sort of metallic colour, about a metre and a half wide, two metres long and about a metre above the green wheat in the field. At first I was trying to rationalize the situation and what the objects were and I thought they might be scientific test equipment that was statically positioned in the field. I then thought for a moment that they were some form of radio controlled object. And

Unidentified flying object at Boreham Down
(Photo: Pierre Beake)

then the next thought came into my mind as to why the crop would be broken down in the field when there's obviously tractor trails for the tractor to drive through, so why would the farmer be breaking the crop down? Yet what was very obvious [was] that there were three distinct trails in the wheat behind the craft, as I call them, that moved down the field. And the wheat was depressed by about 30 cm below the top of the rest of the wheat. And that was very distinct compared with the crop that was around in the rest of the field.

After realizing that I was looking at something that I couldn't explain, and [that] I'd never seen the likes of the objects before, I made several decisions in my mind, to get off my bike and walk up the track here where I could have got very, very close to one of them, because it was only on the edge of the crop. Every time I went to make that decision, something entered my head saying: "Don't go and walk up the track. Leave us alone. It's none of your business!" That was exactly the form it took in my mind. I also had a cell phone with me, and I considered a couple of times taking that out and taking a few photographs. But every time

I made that decision, the same feeling came into my head, which is completely out of character with my personality, because I wanted to find out what they were.

I literally sat on my bike for three or four minutes watching. After about half that time the craft which was creeping down the field through the wheat very, very slowly - and I should qualify that they weren't on the ground, they were hovering in the top of the wheat, gliding through it - they were moving very, very slowly for about two minutes, then I felt this feeling come on that they had become aware of me, and I'd become aware, obviously, of them.

Two days afterwards someone said to me: "Have you seen the new crop circle on the Alton Barnes road?". And I said: "Oh, where is that?" And they said: "Well, it's right where you go cycling, underneath West Woods". When they told me that, I had an incredible replay or rerunning of that evening's experience in my mind, to the point where I instantly knew that my thoughts and decision making had been influenced by an outside force. (...) I felt physically ill because I knew I had sort of been duped or, if you like, controlled. I tried to be careful about how it affected me, because it did have a big effect at the time. And I'm very conscious of people that have had experiences like that that have completely changed their life, and that have become slave to the experience and let it dominate their future thinking. I haven't done that. But what (...) I am absolutely sure in my own mind (...) is the fact that some other intelligence is either on this planet or visiting this planet.

The crop circle pictured on page 102 was reported on 22nd June, the morning after Booth had seen the strange objects in the field. It was in the same field and about 200m away from the tracks. When Booth heard about the crop formation, he went straight back to the location and took pictures of the field and the trails made by the 'craft'. He also took samples of the stalks in the trails, which turned out to be bent at the apical nodes. The samples showed that the bent nodes on the stems from the trails were significantly longer than the same nodes on the corn stalks outside the tracks. (Toftenes and author's interview with Mike Booth, July 2006).

Some months after Mike Booth had made his observations and illustrations of the unknown objects, Norwegian crop circle enthusiast Signe Einseth was looking in various archives for pictures of UFOs. She was quite surprised to find on UFO

Sweden's website a picture of an object which seemed very much to resemble the objects Booth had seen. When Booth got to see the picture, he was in fact astonished at the resemblance, which he confirmed, and was very happy that such a photo existed.

The picture at the bottom of page 102 was taken by Kåre Kårevall in 1956 when on a fishing trip to the island of Marskär near Stockholm. He was about to photograph the pike his friend had just caught, when a luminous object lifted off from the ground nearby. Kårevall recounts that he turned quickly towards the object and managed to take a photo of it before it rose into the air and disappeared (UFO Sweden).

However, this was not the end of events at Boreham Down in the summer of 2005. In August, French film producer and UFO specialist Pierre Beake was in Wiltshire to look at crop circles. On the 4th of the month Beake and his wife visited Boreham Down, as usual taking many photos both of the crop circle and the surrounding countryside. Beake has made it a habit to take plenty of photos in all directions when visiting crop circles, having learnt that unidentified objects can often be seen in the skies above the formations when he examines his photos afterwards. Beake has published many photos of such UFOs at www.coldevence.com. One of the pictures he took that afternoon shows a strange object. Beake was standing inside the crop circle at Boreham Down and pointing the camera in a south-westerly direction towards the spinney at Boreham Wood. The photograph shows an unidentified object hanging over the trees. The object is clearly metallic and seems to be horseshoe-shaped (author's interview with Pierre Beake, July 2008).

EXTRA-TERRESTRIAL SOURCES?

Up till now, few people who have studied crop circles over a period of time have considered it probable that crop circles are some kind of landing marks made directly by physical UFOs. Few earlier eye witness accounts have pointed this way, but the occurrences in Poland in 2001 and 2003 mean that we must see that the crop circle phenomenon is perhaps more complex than we have thought up till now.

Still, many people believe that crop circles are made by other civilisations in the universe, without the aliens needing to land on Earth in order to make them. They have wondered if the balls of light could be a sort of probe sent out to make the crop circles. Others tend rather to believe that the circles have their origins on our own planet and that the Earth itself and the special energies of certain places are capable of creating crop circles without any extraterrestrial assistance. Others maintain that our collective unconscious might be creating the crop circles, or that they could be a message from another time or another dimension. Still others believe that 'God' or the 'creative forces of nature' are responsible for them. Some have suggested that different crop circles might come from different sources. Two very special crop formations which appeared in England in 2001 and 2002 do suggest that at least some formations have extra-terrestrial origins (see pp. 163–166).

WHIRLWINDS AND PLASMA VORTICES

Terence Meaden, meteorologist and atmospheric physicist, was one of the first to investigate the crop circle phenomenon systematically. He was particularly intrigued by eye witness reports which suggested that crop circles had been made by whirlwinds. He maintained that it is was a known phenomenon that local whirlwinds could arise on hot, still summer days, especially in the lee of steep hillsides. Such whirlwinds, Meaden claimed, can take the form of funnels, pillars or balls. He also said that whirlwinds can become electrically charged (ionised) and that in such cases it is possible for them to emit both sounds and light. He called such electrically charged whirlwinds 'plasma vortices'.

During the 1980s, Meaden developed a theory that if the spin of such vortices becomes unstable, the funnel can collapse and be drawn electrostatically towards the ground, for example towards a cornfield that has the opposite charge to the plasma vortex. By this mechanism, argued Meaden, the corn could be laid down in swirled circles. When quintuplets started appearing, Meaden added that in some cases whirlwinds have been reported in groups, a main one surrounded by several smaller ones (Meaden 1991, pp. 30–34).

Meaden was determined to find a scientific explanation for the crop circle phenomenon. As long as the crop formations mainly consisted of simple circles and rings, they could be fitted into his plasma vortex model. However, when in the 1990s crop formations began developing more complex patterns, his theories were no longer able to explain them away as a natural phenomenon. He renounced the plasma vortex as a false trail and withdrew from crop circle research.

Other researchers however, such as biophysicist William Levengood of the BLT Research Team in the USA, found the plasma theory worth following up. Levengood uses traditional scientific methods. He suggests that the light phenomena seen when crop circles form, including balls of light and columns of light, might be plasma vortices. He asserts that the plasma vortex theory can explain changes found by BLT in the corn and in soil samples taken from crop circles. However he has no suggestions as to how plasma vortices might be able to produce the very complex patterns which are typical of today's crop formations. We shall return to BLTs research results and theories in chapter 6.

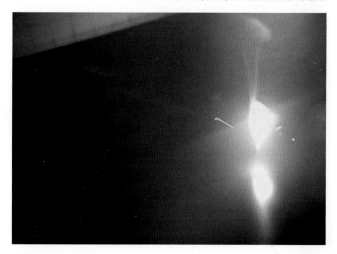

Fireball created in a lab in Brazil in 2007
(Photo: Gerson Paiva)

WHIRLWINDS IN MYTH AND LEGEND

In the East, whirlwinds have traditionally been seen as manifestations of 'jinn' or genies, the supernatural creatures of Arabic and Islamic folklore. In the West also it was usual in olden times to see whirlwinds as a manifestation of spirits or fairies. Were 'fairies' and 'elves' perhaps just concepts people used to describe the same phenomena which now we characterise as whirlwinds, plasma vortices or balls of light?

Could it be that the following story from 17th century England expresses how most people experienced whirlwinds? This account is from John Aubrey's book A Natural History of Wiltshire, published in 1847:

In the year 1633-4, soon after I had entered into my grammar at the Latin School of Yatton Keynal, our curate, Mr. Hart, was annoyed one night by these elves or fayries coming over these downes, it being nearly darke, approaching one of the fairy dances as the common people call them in these parts, viz. the green circles made by those spirits on the grasse, he all at once saw an innumerable quantitie of pigmies or very small people dancing rounde and rounde and singing and making all manner of odd noyses. So being very greatly amaz'd, and yet not being able, as he says, to run away from them, being as he supposes kepte there in a kinde of enchantment. They no sooner perceive him but they surrounde him on all sides, and what betwixt feare and amazement, he fell downe scarecely knowing what he did; and thereupon these little creatures pinche'd him all over, and made a sort of quick humming noyse all the time; but at length they left him, and when the sun rose he found himself exactly in the midst of one of these faery dances.

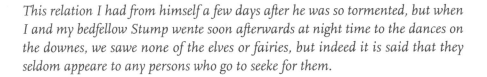

This relation I had from himself a few days after he was so tormented, but when I and my bedfellow Stump wente soon afterwards at night time to the dances on the downes, we sawe none of the elves or fairies, but indeed it is said that they seldom appeare to any persons who go to seeke for them.

Meaden points out that there are many features in this story which remind him of modern accounts of crop circles forming where whirlwinds have been involved. Fairies whirling or dancing round could be seen as an expression of the whirlwind spinning round. The fairies' song and the strange humming noise remind us of the sounds people refer to when they experience whirlwinds today. Fairies pinching him all over the body might perhaps resemble the pricking feeling one gets when one is exposed to an electromagnetic field. Being unable to move as if bewitched is perhaps an expression for what we would today call an altered state of consciousness (Meaden 1991 p.184).

Robert Hunt writes in *Romances of the West of England*: "In some places, whirlwinds are experienced as the presence of fairies, or are seen as signs that fairies are passing by." (Hunt 1881). Another folk-tale recorded by Sir Walter Scott in 1802 in his first book, *Minstrelsy of the Scottish Border*, perhaps refers to both whirlwinds and crop circles:

The fairies of Scotland (...) inhabit the interior of green hills, chiefly those of conical form (...) on which they lead their dances by moon-light; impressing upon the surface the mark of circles, which sometimes appear yellow and blasted, sometimes of a deep green hue; and within which it is dangerous to sleep, or to be found after sunset.

How then might 'plasma vortices' be able to create complex crop circle patterns? Are such vortices perhaps some kind of physical manifestation of a spiritual being, as was believed in times gone by? Levengood suggests that balls of light are actually small plasma vortices. Some people who have experienced balls of light say that they felt a sort of presence, and that the balls of light seem to have a will, intention or intelligence. Can plasma vortices have consciousness, or is it rather the case that balls of light are a sort of probe sent out by an alien intelligence? Others are more inclined to believe that with our unconscious minds we are able to communicate with natural phenomena such as 'plasma vortices' and thus to make them create patterns in corn fields.

PLASMA RESEARCH

Can science throw any light on these historical accounts and perhaps on the contemporary 'spiritual' explanations as well? Certainly plasma research is currently a fast growing field. As we have seen, luminous and glowing balls of light are often observed when crop circles are formed and in association with crop circles. Scientists have succeeded in recent years in creating plasma vortices in the laboratory and have made a connection with ball lightning. We know that ball lightning is also a plasma phenomenon, and in some cases there is evidence to suggest that ball lightning produced in the lab spins around its own axis. The theory is winning ground that balls of light, plasma vortices and ball lightning are all aspect of the same phenomenon. Since 2006, physicists Eli Jerby and Vladimir Dikhtar at Tel Aviv University have been creating a kind of fireball in the laboratory, using a form of 'microwave drill' which they originally developed in order to make holes in non-metallic solids such as glass. The drill melted a hole in the material and when it was withdrawn, super-heated material followed in the form of a pillar of fire, which then collapsed into an elastic ball of light. The strongly glowing balls of light or fireballs were seen to float and bounce around inside the metal chambers which housed the experiments. Many people have repeated these experiments since and have found that fireballs up to several cm in diameter are sustained as long as the microwave power is on, but disappear after 10 to 30 milliseconds once it is switched off. They have some features in common with ball lightning and both are now believed to consist of a cloud of energized nanoparticles, which can be derived from pretty much any material once it is heated over about 700°C, including metals, salts, carbon and water. The open question that remains is how such a fireball or plasma vortex can be sustained outside a metal chamber and with no obvious electromagnetic force to contain it (Abrahamson & Dinniss 2000, Dikhtyar 2006).

In January 2007, Hazel Muir writing in the New Scientist magazine reported on another experiment carried out by António Pavão and Gerson Paiva from the Federal University of Pernambuco in Brazil, in an attempt to see whether lightning striking silicon particles in the soil could be responsible for the creation of ball lightning: *[The researchers] took wafers of silicon just 350 micrometres thick, placed them between two electrodes and zapped them with currents of up to 140 amps. Then over a couple of seconds, they moved the electrodes slightly apart, creating an electrical arc that vaporised the silicon. The arc spat out glowing fragments of silicon but also, sometimes, luminous orbs the size of ping-pong balls that persisted for up to 8 seconds. "The luminous balls seem to be alive," says*

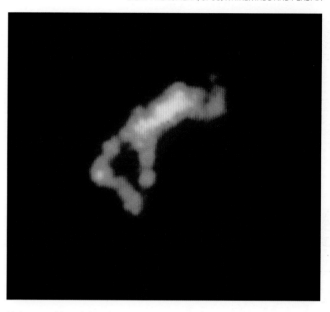

Lights over Hessdalen photographed in 1982 (Photo: Arne Thomassen)

Unidentified light over Hessdalen photographed in 1982
(Photo: Leif Havik)

Pavão. He says their fuzzy surfaces emitted little jets that seemed to jerk them forward or sideways, as well as smoke trails that formed spiral shapes, suggesting the balls were spinning. From their blue-white or orange-white colour, Paiva's team estimates that they have a temperature of roughly 1700C. The balls were able to melt plastic, and one even burned a hole in Paiva's jeans. (Muir 2007).

As we have seen, luminous and glowing balls of light are often observed when crop circles are formed and in association with crop circles. The experiments carried out by the Brazilian and Israeli scientists may be able to add new dimensions of understanding to these observations. Crop circle researchers have noticed that the nodes of the corn stalks in the flattened corn are often elongated or even exploded. William Levengood and the BLT Research Team have succeeded in reproducing these effects in the lab by exposing corn stalks to short period of intense microwave radiation. Another study has shown that the relationship between oxygen and nitrogen in the soil in crop circles is changed in the same way that the soil is changed where lightning strikes.

Countless visitors to crop circles have had problems with technical equipment in freshly made crop circles. Cameras, camcorders, sound recorders, computers and mobile phones have stopped working or have behaved abnormally. Jeffrey Wilson's research organisation ICCRA has shown increased levels of electromagnetism and of radioactivity in fresh crop circles, and he thinks that this can be attributed to microwave radiation. Levels return to normal within about ten days.

According to scientists, certain plasma phenomena emit microwaves. Several witnesses have reported that an intense heat is associated with the formation of crop circles. This heat would cause changes in the corn and the soil. But the heat must be very short-lived, probably only lasting a fraction of a second, since it is very rare to find any burn marks on the corn.

THE LIGHT PHENOMENA OF HESSDALEN

It's not just in England that strange light phenomena are observed. The residents of the valley of Hessdalen in Norway, near the copper-mining town of Røros, have for generations past observed mysterious light phenomena which in some cases share features with the balls of light seen in Wiltshire corn-fields. Scientists working on the Hessdalen lights in recent years have also come to the conclusion that they are dealing with a plasma phenomenon.

In the 1980s the Hessdalen lights were observed so frequently - up to 20 times a week - that they caught the attention of scientists and the media. The lights were typically amorphous, bright white or yellow and apparently floating in the air, often high in the night sky. Sometimes flickering, sometimes steady, they seemed to appear from nowhere and disappear as mysteriously. The observations led to many speculations, and the media mostly ridiculed the whole thing. Some researchers, however, took another stand. A handful of them, with university professor and civil engineer Erling Strand in the lead, established a permanent research station in the middle of the valley. Since 1983 they have been collecting data in the form of photographs and scientific recordings. The operation was given the name Project Hessdalen and continues to this day, now with the assistance and collaboration of the Italian National Research Council, which set up an automatic monitoring station in 1998 to relay data to the Institute for Radio Astronomy in Bologna. A huge amount of data has been collected and the different coloured lights have been recorded moving around over the mountains and ridges which surround the valley, often at impressive speeds and with rapid changes of course. One light was clocked by radar moving at 30,000 kilometres an hour (48,000 mph), but the lights also move slowly, stop and sometimes divide into several parts. Their size varies but they can be as big as a house (Project Hessdalen).

In 2007, Professor Bjørn Gitle Hauge, also working with the Hessdalen project, published a set of results from the monitoring programme which mean that we now have a good idea what the lights are composed of. Spectrographic analysis and electromagnetic measurements have shown that they consist of a burning vortex of gas or plasma, with a light output of up to a megawatt. Apart from the elements present in normal air, such as oxygen and nitrogen, silicon and the more unusual element scandium have also been recorded in the spectra. Scandium is a rare earth type of metal which is found as its oxide in several minerals, but with by far the greatest quantities in thortveitite, discovered in Norway.

But how do these balls of incandescent gas arise, where do they come from and how do they maintain their integrity rather than just burning up or dispersing immediately? Professor Hauge and his colleagues have said that when they find the answer to these questions, we may be a step nearer to solving the energy problems of the future, as the Hessdalen lights are thought to contain huge amounts of energy.

Lights over Hessdalen, 2007. The coloured bars underneath are a spectrographic image of the same lights (Bjørn Gitle Hauge/ Project Hessdalen)

CHAPTER 5

CROP CIRCLES ON THE GROUND

The geometrical patterns and beautiful artistic designs of the crop circles can only really be appreciated from the air. However, to actually go into a crop circle in the field is to experience a whole new dimension of the phenomenon. This chapter is dedicated to the beauty of crop circles on the ground. I'd like to present to you some crop circles with features worth taking a closer look at. Some of these I was lucky enough to visit myself while they were still fresh. In other cases we will have to be content with other researchers' descriptions and photographs.

When one enters a new formation, the first thing one notices is the beauty of the lay: how the corn is swirled and flattened and how it often flows water-like from one section to another. Sometimes there will be smaller circles not crossed by the tramlines or linked to the rest of the pattern, seemingly placed there by magic, with no signs of footprints or other means of access. In some cases the corn can be bent higher up rather than at the base of the stalks, so that the laid corn 'floats' above the ground. In addition to beautiful whirls and flowing lay, one can find corn which is braided, twisted, woven and knotted in astonishing ways. In other cases one can come across three-dimensional constructions in the corn, almost like birds' nests or elaborately styled hair-dos.

Facing page: Inside the formation at East Kennet, 2008
(Photo: Eva-Marie Brekkestø)

FIRST INTO A NEW CIRCLE

On 8th July 2008, after several days in Wiltshire with no new crop circle reports due to dreadful weather, at last a new formation is spotted. I'm visiting the local airstrip at Yatesbury when I learn that a micro light pilot, after many days of strong winds and rain, has finally managed to get airborne and has spotted a new formation. He shows me on the map where he thinks the circle is, near to East Kennet only a couple of miles away, and I head off to find it. It takes me a few hours to comb the countryside. It's a special feeling to walk the fields on one's own like this. The corn is still green and lush at this time of the year, and the sun is lovely and warm when it breaks through the gaps in the clouds. When at last I find the formation, I understand why no one else has discovered it from the ground. It's placed on the top of a rise, a good distance from the nearest road, and can't be seen from any of the paths in the area either. When I get inside, I feel truly privileged to witness such pristine beauty. The laid corn is wound playfully around 40 tiny circles of standing corn. The completely undamaged corn stalks, bent at a height of 10–15 cm above the ground, flow elegantly in all directions and create beautiful whirls and spirals. Later I learn that from the air the unusual pattern looks like a necklace with an oval pendant.

VISITING CROP CIRCLES

First-time visitors to crop circles are often surprised by their beauty at ground level, especially before too many people have trampled the corn flat. The lay can be very airy and dynamic. The plant stems flow like water in elegant streams and whirls, gracefully changing direction while following the elements of the pattern. When the stalks are not flattened to the ground but float several centimetres above it, it feels like sacrilege to step into the circle and tread them down. Many people feel a sense of wonder and awe when they stand in front of a virgin crop circle. Some take off their shoes and go barefoot. Corn circle enthusiast Karen Alexander expressed this attitude of reverence nicely when she coined the phrase "Temporary Temples".

But, if we want to visit new crop circles, it's impossible to avoid damaging them to some degree. For every step we take into the formation, we hear the crunching sounds of corn being crushed to the ground. All we can do is to move around the formations with the utmost care, so that they are as little spoilt as possible for the visitors who will

Facing page: The whole circle at East Kennet 2008
(Photo: Eva-Marie Brekkestø)

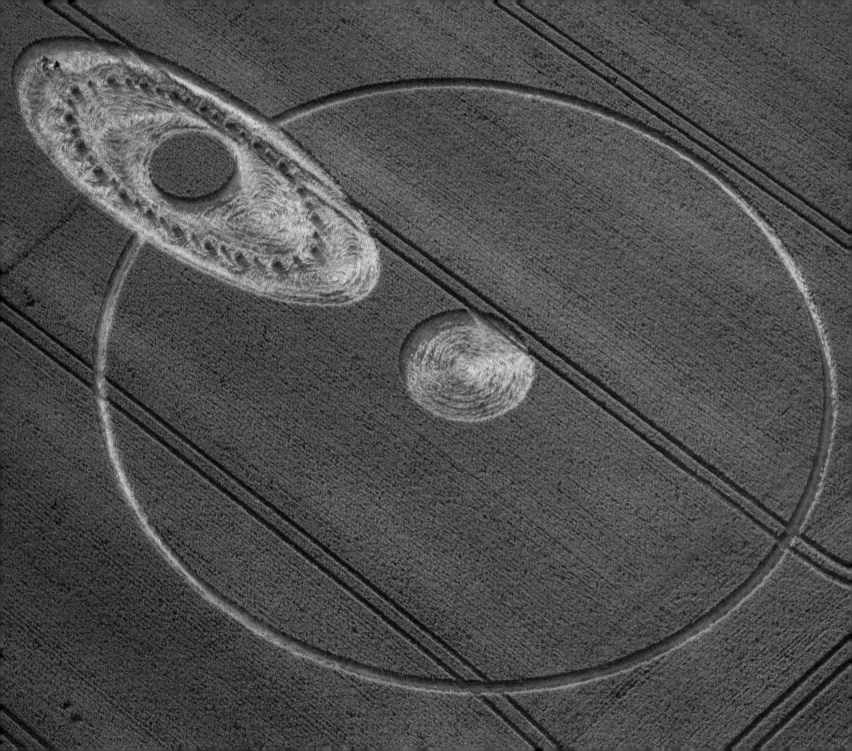

come after us. Seasoned crop circle enthusiasts have suggested that respect for the crop circles and for our fellow human beings would be best expressed if we all followed a Code of Conduct:

1) Never walk through the standing corn. This is guaranteed to annoy the farmer and if will also spoil the pattern. Follow the tram-lines (parallel tracks left by the tractor when spraying with pesticides) into the field. If you've chosen the wrong tram-line, you may have to go back to the edge of the field in order to get in to the right one, which can be annoying when the formation is only a few metres in front of you. The temptation to cross over can be great. But there is only one thing to do: take a deep breath, follow the tram-lines out again and think of the healthy extra exercise you are getting!

2) When you get into the formation, be careful where you put your feet, and avoid trampling any fine details of the lay or pattern which others would like to see.

3) Don't walk right into the centres. Look at the beautiful swirls and other fine details from a little distance. And please, don't sit or lie down in the centre of a fresh crop circle! Leave the beauty intact for others to enjoy later!

4) Sometimes it's not possible to get into parts of a crop formation without trampling through standing corn. In that case, just accept that you can't go in there and that you have to look at and photograph these parts from a small distance.

5) If you find a crop circle with a really unusual lay, be satisfied with standing on the edge of the pattern. Don't go in if it means you will trample the details to bits.

On 17th July 2008, a new formation was reported at West Woods near the village of Lockeridge in Wiltshire, a large and striking cross-shaped pattern with four snaking arms. At the centre of the formation was a circle of flattened corn eight metres across, surrounded by a two metre wide ring of standing corn, so that one could not get into the centre without going through the standing corn. In most crop circles there are small openings into all parts of the pattern, either by virtue of the design of the pattern itself or via the tram-lines, but not in this case. The first visitors to the West Woods formation

Left: The formation at West Woods photographed on 20th July 2009 (Photo: Eva-marie Brekkestø)
Above: Detail form the same formation photographed on 17th July showing the intact central ring (Photo: Bert Janssen)

respected the fact that there was no way into the centre, and did not force their way in. Bert Janssen, one of the early visitors, took a beautiful pole shot showing that at that stage nobody had damaged the ring of standing corn around the centre. Three days later, when I photographed the formation from the air, several paths leading into the centre space had been made. On the photo above you can in fact see a group of people lying in the centre of the crop circle. However, it was not this group which caused the damage; they only followed the many paths through the standing corn which had already been made by that stage.

SOME NOTEWORTHY FORMATIONS

On the 9th August 1994, a very unusual crop circle was discovered in a wheatfield at Markim near Vallentuna, twenty-five miles (40 km) north of Stockholm. The formation consisted of a simple circle 14 metres in diameter, but what made it perhaps the most remarkable Swedish crop circle ever was the very special lay. The wheat seemed to be fluffed up into an elegant whirl, with the stalks arranged into

Top: Crop circle near Vallentuna, Sweden 1994 (photo Clas Svahn)
Above: Detail of crop circle near Vallentuna 1994 (Photo: Clas Svahn)
Opposite page: "The Basket", Bishops Cannings, Wiltshire, August 1999
(Photo and copyright: Ulrich Kox)

springy swathes bent 10–15 cm above the ground, almost as if it had been parted with a giant comb. Notice also that the corn must have begun to fall along a radius and then continued to go down in a sweeping angular movement somewhat like a fan being opened.

Clas Svahn has for many years been a leading figure in Swedish UFO research and is chairman of the group UFO Sweden. In 1998 he published a book about UFOs and crop circles, in which he makes no secret of the fact that he thinks that most Swedish and other crop circles are man-made. Nevertheless he admits that this Swedish circle was something quite special and hard to explain away (Svahn 1998, and in telephone conversation with the author 2009).

1999 BISHOPS CANNINGS, WILTSHIRE, ENGLAND

This fantastic crop circle was discovered on 6th August 1999 by the German crop circle enthusiast Ulrich Kox, who was out for an early morning flight in the area with a micro light. He took the only known aerial shots of this formation. As he flew over it, he could clearly see how special the lay was, so as soon as he landed, he got in touch with two colleagues and asked them to go and take a closer look at the amazing formation on the ground. Experienced crop circle researchers Andreas Müller and Werner Anderhub set off immediately and found a relatively modest sized circle (just over 50 m in diameter) containing 28 slender rings of standing corn, arranged in seven radii fanning out from a central ring. The rings, of progressively increasing diameters, each enclosed beautiful dynamic whirls of flattened crop, while through the rest of the formation the background was composed entirely of flattened corn which had been literally woven together; hence its nickname 'the basket'. Müller and Anderhub managed to measure the formation and take some photos of the unique lay. But already at 10 a.m. the same morning, the furious farmer arrived on his combine harvester to destroy the circle, which he described as 'vandalism in the fields'. Other enthusiasts had now turned up and tried in vain to stop the farmer as he drove his combine into the field. The same afternoon, the Dutch author and film producer Bert Janssen arrived on site with his camera to film the sorry remains of the formation. As he stood there filming the sad spectacle of the circular patch of stubble, he caught something quite unexpected on tape: a little ball of light which took off from the ground within the destroyed formation and flew up and out of the

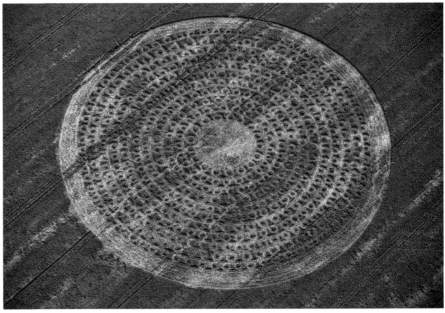

OAbove: Detail of the circle at North Down, July 2003
(Photo: William Betts)
Right: North Down July 2003 (Photo: Bert Janssen)

field (Müller 2001 and Ulrich Kox in conversation with the author 2003).

2003 NORTH DOWN, WILTSHIRE

The Wiltshire countryside is adorned with thousands of late Bronze Age and early Iron Age burial mounds, and these are especially numerous in the areas around Avebury and Stonehenge.

The mounds, also known as tumuli, are usually about 3 to 5 metres in height and have a diameter of up to 25 metres.

On the 6th July 2003 a crop circle was discovered in a very special placement within the archaeological landscape. On North Down, a few miles south west of Avebury, a row of four ancient tumuli was extended by the arrival of a new crop circle in alignment with the others. As well as its special placement, the formation, made in green unripe barley, featured a very detailed design and a highly original lay. The pattern was made up of about 500 small swirled doughnuts of lightly flattened corn, tightly packed together and arranged in 11 concentric rings, with a circle of standing crop in the centre of each doughnut and with standing crop in the wedge-shaped areas between the doughnuts.

2003 WEST STOWELL, WILTSHIRE

A strikingly beautiful crop circle appeared at West Stowell Farm in the Vale of Pewsey on the 20th July 2003. The pattern, a thirteen-pointed star, would be very difficult geometry to construct on paper, never mind in a cornfield during the hours of darkness! The design was similar to a known Mayan symbol. However, it wasn't just the geometry which was impressive with this crop circle, but also the special details of the lay.

We heard about this formation the same day it was discovered and were told that it was especially interesting. We set off excitedly to visit it, but that would prove to be easier said than done. West Stowell Farm is rather isolated and can only be reached via narrow country lanes. To get to the land itself, you have to drive through the farmyard first. The farm manager and farm workers there were keeping a close watch and letting no-one through to the crop circle. We reconnoitred around the area and saw what we could from nearby paths and vantage points such as Golden Ball Hill.

The desire to get into the formation grew. Finally, towards evening, we decided we had to try to sneak in. All seemed quiet at the farm, so we crept carefully into the field. We got so far as to see some unusual and exciting details of the lay and to take a few quick snaps before an angry farm worker appeared and shouted at us to get out of the field. The next day we decided on a different strategy. We approached the manager in his office and, on our very best manners, we managed to reach an agreement with him: we would be allowed to enter the circle under his personal supervision and together with a couple of other crop circle researchers and photographers, and in return we would ask our contacts at the Crop Circle Connector website to publicise the farmer's request for a total ban on further visitors.

The farmer was very surprised at what he saw when he accompanied us to the formation. The day before, he had explained that he didn't understand what all the fuss was about since everyone knew that crop circles were all made by pranksters. But now he was singing another tune! There before us was an immaculate crop circle. The laid crop in between the jewel-like polygons which made up the pattern was perfect, fresh and flowing throughout. In each of the inner 13 spaces a special feature

Wreath of braided corn, detail of the circle at West Stowell, 2003
(Photo: Eva-Marie Brekkestø)

Above: Detail of the circle at Wilton Windmill 2004
(Photo: Janet Ossebaard)
Right: Wilton Windmill 2004 (Photo: Bert Janssen)
Facing page: West Stowell 2003 (Photo: Bert Janssen)

about a metre in diameter had been constructed in the laid crop: a circle of corn stalks had been bent 15cm above ground and twisted together in an anticlockwise direction to make a small raised ring, at the centre of which was a tightly bundled knot made of the rest of the available corn stalks. In two of other areas of laid crop, there was another type of special feature: small circles composed of 7 small sheaves of knotted-together corn, with an eighth marking the centre.

Even the farmer was clearly impressed with this fabulous display of crop circle art, and he seemed very interested in the discussions between the experts present. When we got back to the farmyard, the farmer asked us into his office. There he told us that they had had many fine crop circles on the farm over the years, and showed us pictures of them as well as of formations on other farms nearby. The farmer revealed that he had actually been convinced for many years that crop circles are not man-made, but that he couldn't admit that to the world at large. And then came the most surprising revelation: "We have strict orders from Lady Rothschild, who owns the land here, that no-one is allowed to visit the crop circle. She is coming down to look at it herself in a few days' time".

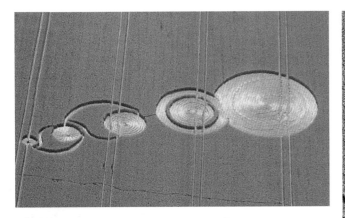

Top: Garsington 2005 (Photo: Andrew King)
Above: Garsington 2005, detail (Photo: Eva-Marie Brekkestø)
Facing page: Garsington 2005, detail (Photo: Axel Kayser)

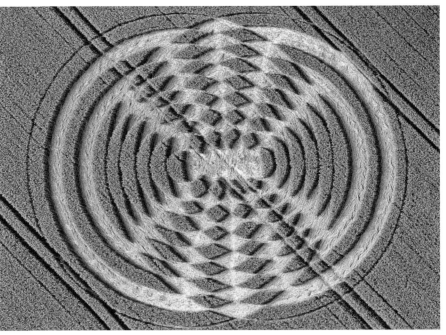

2004 WILTON WINDMILL, WILTSHIRE

This circle was found in the village of Wilton in east Wiltshire, much visited on account of its restored working windmill. The formation appeared on 7th August 2004 in the field next to the windmill. It showed six-fold symmetry, based on a central standing hexagon and a laid six-pointed star. In the centre of the formation, a small circle of laid crop featured a beautiful and special three-dimensional lay, in which the corn was twisted into a rope-like ridge spiralling tightly in to the centre (Janet Ossebaard in conversation with the author).

2005 GARSINGTON, OXFORDSHIRE

When crop circle enthusiast Andrew King flew over the village of Garsington just outside Oxford on the 15th July 2005, he spotted a crop circle with a not particularly impressive design, a simple row of circles in fact. However he did also notice that the circles seemed to have an interesting lay. A few days later I drove up to Oxfordshire

to try and find the formation on the ground, in the company of Guro Parvanova and Axel Kayser. We spent two hours searching all around the village, by car and on foot, and were about to give up. The location given on Crop Circle Connector must have been totally wrong, we decided.

In a final effort before leaving, we looked for a nearby vantage point, and drove up to Denton Lane. From there we examined carefully with binoculars the fields to the north of Garsington. We caught sight of a small shadow on a field half hidden behind a hedge. Eagerly we drove back and made our way into the field - to our surprise, one which we had already searched without finding anything! The field sloped upwards away from the road before falling away again towards a hollow at the other end, thus concealing the formation from view.

The sight which greeted us when we went into the formation made us go weak at the knees. Laughing and crying by turns, we fired off hundred of photos. We just couldn't believe what we were seeing. Lined up in a row were five circles, with no signs of anyone else having visited them. The corn-stalks in the southernmost and largest, about 23 m in diameter, were plaited in a spiral pattern from the edge into the middle. In the next two circles, 15 m and 10 m in diameter, the corn was formed into swath-like ridges 20 cm high and 30 cm wide, also spiralling into the centre. Every stalk was precisely placed in these swaths. We were awe-struck, and avoided going into the circles for fear of destroying the lay. Two further circles, about 7 m and 3.5 m in diameter, left us equally speechless. Here all the corn seemed to have been blown from the edges towards the centre, where it met in a tangled tussock of stalks as if waves crashing against each other had frozen in mid-air. Guro caught sight of a shadow further down the field and went to check it out. We soon followed when we heard her shout with delight, "Three more circles!"

Two tramlines further down towards the bottom of the field, we came first to two mini-circles about one metre in diameter. In the first, the corn-stalks were twisted together half-way up the stem, then splayed out towards the edges again. The second was a beautiful small whirl. Just a little further down the slope, we came to the last three circles. The two largest (about 8m and 6.5m in diameter) had the same spiral construction as the second and third circles in the upper part of the formation, only even more elegantly made. These two circles of laid crop overlapped each other, with the edge of the one circle still defined within the overlap by an arc of only one stalk's width. The eighth and final circle was another whirl, just one and half metres in diameter. As we were photographing it, the sun broke through the clouds and gave us some fine last shots of the formation in the beautiful evening light.

The formation at Garsington felt like sacred ground, like a sort of temple, and neither I nor my friends considered going into the circles. We didn't discuss it at the time, it simply never occurred to us to touch or walk into the laid crop. We spent a few hours there just looking, taking photos and feeling grateful that we had had the chance to experience such a wonder before it got destroyed by other visitors, as we feared might happen. To this very day I am still amazed that we didn't even reach into the edge of the circles to examine the laid crop more closely, as I normally would do when visiting a crop circle.

When we showed our pictures to other friends back in Wiltshire the same evening, we realised that a lot of people would be heading out to Garsington the next day. However, it rained heavily all the next day, and when the influx of visitors made it up there the day after, they were disappointed to find that the unique lay had mostly collapsed under the weight of the rain. We felt even more grateful then that we'd been lucky enough to find this jewel of a formation, and that we'd been able to photograph it in all its glory before it was lost.

2005 MARDEN, WILTSHIRE

This unique crop circle, discovered on the 9th August 2005, aroused a lot of interest. The overall pattern contained familiar elements: four small circles placed on a ring around a larger one to form a 'quintuplet', and then another ring around the whole thing. What made this formation utterly unique was firstly that the lay in the centre was so complex, and secondly that it formed a recognisable pattern. As far as I know, this was the first time that a recognisable symbol had been portrayed in the lay itself, rather than a pattern being defined by means of alternating areas of standing and laid crop. In the centre of the formation, the corn was plaited, woven and knotted together in irregular ridges, swirls, nests and constructions of all sorts. Far from being a random result, this inner pattern was an almost exact reproduction of the Mayan symbol 'Saq'Be'. Saq'Be means 'white way', and refers to the Milky Way and mankind's spiritual development.

This intriguing formation was placed at a location little known for crop circles, near the village of Marden, at the southern edge of the Vale of Pewsey. Marden had not hosted crop circles before, so some people wondered why such a notable crop circle would appear just here. After all, crop circles do tend to appear near to ancient sacred sites such as stone circles, white horses, henges and so on. At Marden there doesn't seem to be anything of any such interest. However, it turns out that in Neolithic times Marden was the site of the largest henge in Britain, bigger even than Avebury! What's more, it contained a huge mound known as Hatfield Barrow, second only to Silbury Hill, which was levelled for farming in the first decade of the 19th century. Remains of the ditch and bank are still visible and the 37 acre site is now being investigated by archaeologists.

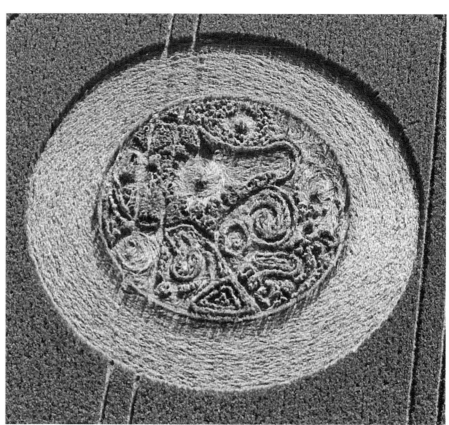

Above: The Mayan symbol Saq'Be
Right: The centre of the formation at Marden 2005
(Photo: Steve Alexander)
Facing page: Marden 2005 (Photo: Steve Alexander)

Above, right: Detail at ground level of the Marden 2005 circle
(Photo: Charles Mallett)
Top: Detail at ground level of the Marden 2005 circle
(Photo: Annemieke Witteveen)
Above: Detail at ground level of the Marden 2005 circle
(Photo: Annemieke Witteveen)

2005 ALDBOURNE, ENGLAND

This crop circle, which appeared on 24th July, had an unusual and complex pattern arranged around a triangle of standing crop in the centre. Numerous different shaped rhomboids and triangles all pointed towards the corners of the triangle as if these were the centres of a magnetic field. The impression of magnetic force was reinforced by the lay itself, as the laid corn near to the corners of the central triangle was twisted tightly together into thick bundles, flowing together in large knots with an 'organic' appearance, almost like the roots of a tree.

2006 WAYLAND'S SMITHY, OXFORDSHIRE

This crop formation appeared on 8th July near the Neolithic passage grave known as Wayland's Smithy, near to Uffington. The strikingly unusual pattern seen in aerial views was thought by many to resemble a cluster of skyscrapers. These 'skyscrapers' were arranged in three groups of four each, ascending in 'height' within each group. On the tallest tower in each group, the flat 'roof' was composed of an unusual lay,

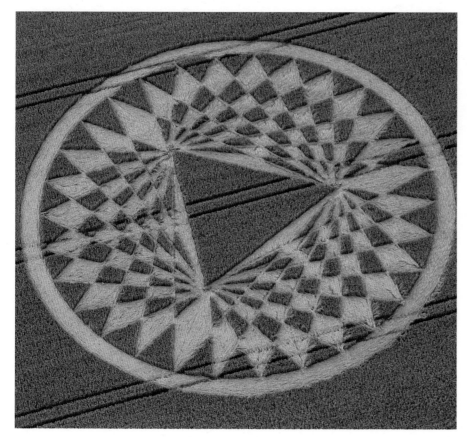

Left: Aldbourne 2005 (Photo: Axel Kayser)
Above: Detail at ground level of the circle near Aldbourne, July 2005
(Photo: Eva-Marie Brekkestø)

in which the corn-stalks were laid in bundles flattened in two opposite directions and passing over and under each other, giving the effect of a woven texture.

2006 CHARLBURY HILL, OXFORDSHIRE

This modest looking crop circle formation appeared on the 11th July 2006, aligned with a small tumulus just by Charlbury Hill. The Ridgeway passes nearby on its traverse of large parts of Wiltshire and Oxfordshire. The formation consisted of three simple circles with rings, and the whole thing was not more than 70 m long. If the pattern was unremarkable, the same could not be said about the lay! The still green

Right: Formation at Wayland's Smithy 2006 (Photo: Terje Toftenes)
Over: Detail, Wayland's Smithy 2006 (Photo: Eva-Marie Brekkestø)

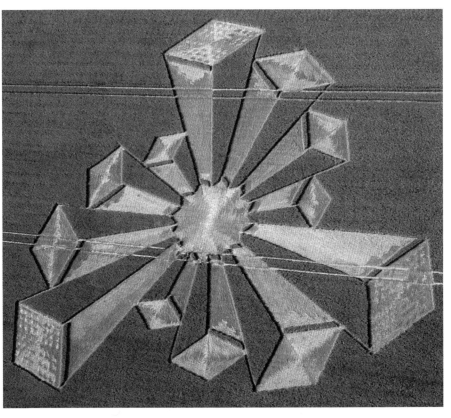

corn was intricately woven in the large central circle, while in the two smaller outer circles it was arranged in hundreds of knotted clusters at knee height.

2007 WHITE'S HILL, RAMSBURY, WILTSHIRE

This formation was found near the village of Ramsbury on 18th July 2007. It was not at one of the usual crop circle hot spots, and was only discovered by someone flying over the area on his way to photograph another formation. Even in England it must be assumed that outside the main crop circle areas, a significant number of formations appear every year which never get reported, simply because no-one spots them before the fields are harvested.

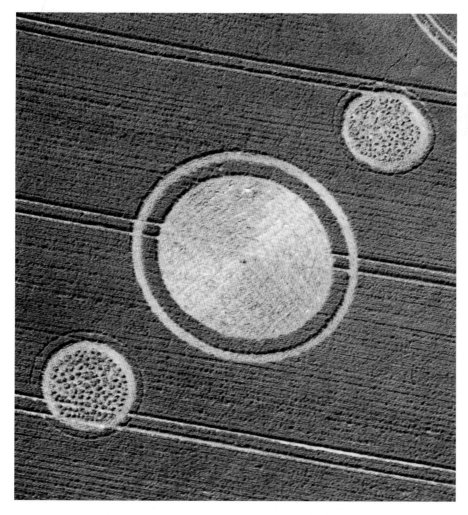

Left: Charlbury Hill, July 2006 (Photo: Terje Toftenes)
Above: Detail, Charlbury Hill 2006 (Photo: Eva-Marie Brekkestø)

The term 'crop circle' was definitely an unsuitable one for this unusual pattern, made up entirely of rectangular shapes! However, the formation, which after a while picked up the nickname of 'the duck' or 'the dog', was very special on the ground. Inside the many rectangles of different sizes, the laid corn ran in the most elegant whirls and streams, flowing uninterruptedly in varying directions. This formation offered something unusual, namely 'square swirls'!

Top: White's Hill 2007 (Photo: Eva-Marie Brekkestø)
Top right and above: Detail, White's Hill 2007
(Photo: Eva-Marie Brekkestø)

2007 HINTON DOWNS, OXFORDSHIRE

This formation appeared on the 16th July 2007 at Hinton Downs, near Swindon, on the Wiltshire / Oxfordshire border, and was like an exhibition of different types of lay. The pattern, an untidy agglomeration of small circles rather like a root of ginger, aroused little attention as it seemed quite uninteresting from the aerial photos. However after some years as a crop circle chaser I have learnt that it is precisely the small and at first sight uninteresting formations which can be very well worth while taking a closer look at. So we made haste to track down this formation as soon as it was reported.

This formation was placed right next to a tumulus, and the first thing which surprised us when we saw it was how the circles seemed to incorporate the burial mound in the design. When we got close, we were delighted to see that the formation was like a display case of the most incredible arrangements of corn-stalks: swirls, knots, rosettes, spirals and constructions of all sorts!

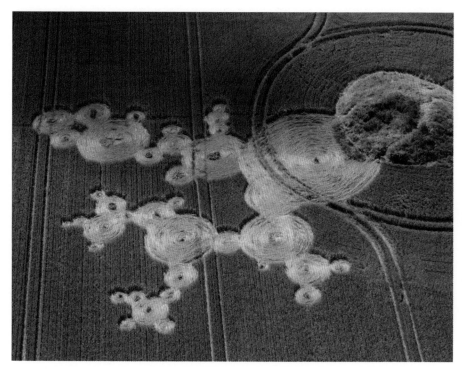

2009 YATESBURY, WILTSHIRE

This special formation appeared in a field of green barley at Yatesbury, just outside Avebury, on 12th June 2009. It looked like a stylized bird emerging from flames, and not surprisingly became known as the Phoenix. On the ground, the young barley was swept and swirled vigorously in constantly changing directions, retaining a wonderful lightness and fluffiness as if the whole pattern had been created using a gigantic hair-dryer. And the formation featured several most unusual sections of *standing* corn stalks which had been swirled (Roy Leraand, in conversation with the author 2009).

Top left: Hinton Downs 2007 (Photo: Axel Kayser)
Above: Detail, Hinton Downs 2007 (Photo: Eva-Marie Brekkestø)

2009 SILBURY HILL, WILTSHIRE

This crop circle had a relatively simple pattern; around a central large circle, two

Top: Yatesbury Phoenix, June 2009 (Photo: Roy Leraand)
Right: Detail, Yatesbury Phoenix, June 2009 (Photo: Charles Mallett)
Above: Detail, Yatesbury Phoenix, June 2009 (Photo: Roy Leraand)

Facing page: Crop circle in flowering oilseed rape, with Avebury in the background, April 2009 (Photo: Eva-Marie Brekkestø)

curving rows of five circles each, of diminishing size, were placed with their centres on an unmarked circle concentric with the first one. On the ground there were a profusion of exciting details in the lay, with knot constructions in the centres, spirals and many fine whirls throughout the whole laid area (Shawn Randall in conversation with the author, 2009).

2010 CLEY HILL, WILTSHIRE, ENGLAND

At the foot of Cley Hill, about 5 km west of Warminster in south-west Wiltshire, a very unusual formation appeared on the 9th July. Framed within a hexagonal outline,

Right: Detail, Silbury Hill August 2009
(Photo: Shawn Randall)

another figure with six fold symmetry was so 'shaded' that it could only be intended as a 3-D figure. From the right angle it was reminiscent of a Rubik's cube with the corner pieces removed. Usually crop circle patterns are created by alternating areas of standing and laid crop, but the 3-D effect of Cley Hill was achieved by 'stippling' areas of the field with both standing and flattened corn at the same time. This in-between state was created with many rows of small clusters of standing corn, with the flattened corn lying crosswise between them.

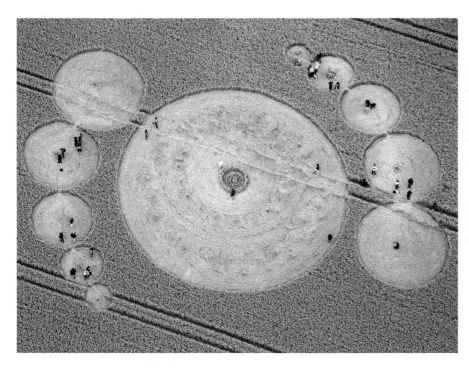

2010 WINDMILL HILL, WILTSHIRE, ENGLAND

On the morning of the 27th July, a new crop circle was reported from Windmill Hill just outside Avebury. Formations in these well-known locations quickly attract a lot of visitors, but luckily I was already nearby and managed to get to the circle while the details on the ground were still undamaged. And what details! The general pattern of the huge formation was a six-leaved rosette surrounded by a ring of 36 circles, with an airy, flowing lay; in the central circle and many of the larger satellite circles were a profusion of elegant centre pieces, with twisted nests, knotted sheaves and other intriguing arrangements of corn. This formation was the summer's absolute highpoint for many crop circle enthusiasts!

CROP CIRCLES IN OILSEED RAPE

Every year, both in England and other countries, a number of circles appear in oilseed

Above left: Silbury Hill, August 2009 (Photo: Olivier Morel)
Top: The 3 D formation at Cley Hill, July 2010 (photo Eva-Marie Brekkestø)
Above: Detail, Cley Hill, July 2010 (photo Eva-Marie Brekkestø)

Top: The six-leaved rosette at Windmill Hill, July 2010.
(Photo: Eva-Marie Brekkestø)
Above: Detail from the centre piece, Windmill Hill July 2010
(Photo: Eva-Marie Brekkestø)

rape (canola) fields. Usually they are seen during the last two weeks of April and the first two weeks of May, when the rape is in flower and the fields are shining bright yellow with their blooms. Oilseed rape formations are interesting because the plant is much more difficult to bend neatly than is corn. The stalks are as thick as a finger, rubbery on the outside and sappy within. It takes force to bend them, and if you persist in pressing them to the ground, you will leave clear signs of the process. For one thing, the stems are likely to snap a few centimetres above the ground. In man-made rapeseed circles, the stalks are often so badly damaged that the flowers wither and die. Such formations look a sorry mess already a few hours after they have been made. For another, anyone treading down the crop or walking over the laid crop will leave muddy footprints on the stems if the soil is at all damp, which it usually is at that time of year. It's very difficult to make precise patterns in oilseed rape anyway, since the plant grows more than a metre and a half in height and is quite bushy compared with corn; all this and its resistance to being bent also makes it hard to control which way any individual stem will fall.

In 2006 at Botley in Oxfordshire, some people tried nevertheless to make a circle in flowering oilseed rape. The pictures from the ground show badly damaged plants. The stems are broken, bruised and muddy from where the hoaxers trampled the plants down. By contrast, the beautiful rapeseed formation which appeared on 1st May 2005 under Golden Ball Hill, next to the famous East Field in the Vale of Pewsey, showed totally undamaged stalks, elegantly bent down to the ground. The plants continued to flower and to grow as normal. If you look closely at the picture of the oilseed rape plants in this circle, taken two days after discovery, you'll see that the laid plants are entirely undamaged and are flowering as nicely as the standing ones!

Left: Golden Ball Hill, May 2005 (Photo: Steve Alexander)
Top: Broken and damaged rape-stalks in the man-made rape circle at
Botley in 2006 (Photo: William Betts)
Above: Undamaged and smoothly bent rape-stalks in the circle at Golden
Ball Hill in May 2005 (Photo: Steve Alexander

CHAPTER 6

CROP CIRCLE SCIENCE AND RESEARCH

In this chapter we're going to look at some research studies, by both amateur enthusiasts and professional scientists, which may throw some light on the forces involved in the creation of crop circles. We will also consider some reports of physical effects on equipment, animals and people which have been associated with crop circles.

RESEARCH INTO CROP CIRCLES

The crop circles are quite different from many other paranormal phenomena because they are easily accessible for scientific research. It's much more of a challenge to study UFOs or ghosts, for example. One never knows when such phenomena will turn up and they don't stay around to be examined physically. Crop circles on the other hand show up in their hundreds every season, and anyone with the farmer's permission can wander in and takes samples of the corn and the soil. And this has in fact been done by different research groups for many years now.

BLT

The BLT Research Team Inc was founded in the early 1990s by John Burke, a New

Facing page: Formation discovered near Chisbury, Wilthire 3rd July 2010
(Photo: Eva-Marie Brekkestø)

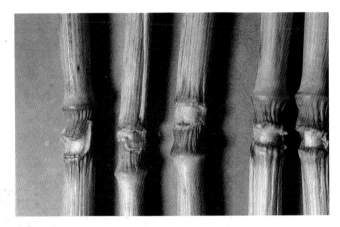

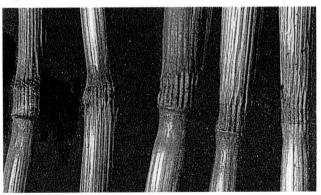

York businessman with a background in physics and agriculture, Michigan biophysicist W.C. Levengood, and Nancy Talbott, a research analyst who organized and funded an international fieldwork effort and became spokesperson for the Team. BLT has examined thousands of plants and soils from more than 250 crop circles in eight different countries. The samples, taken from both flattened and standing crop areas within crop circles were compared to plant and soil controls, taken at various distances outside the flattened areas.   Three papers reporting their crop circle research have been published in peer-reviewed scientific journals. These papers present evidence for the involvement of three different types of energy involved in the creation of crop circles:

- a heating agency (probably microwaves)
- strong magnetic fields
- unusual electrical pulses

I summarize here the most important of their findings. It's impossible to do that without using a certain amount of scientific language, and perhaps too much detail for some readers. Others who would like to go deeper into the research will find all the articles, studies and lab reports http://www.bltresearch.com.

HEAT-PRODUCING ENERGY

Several people who have witnessed a crop circle being formed and have had the chance to go into it have said that the corn was hot for the first few minutes after the circle formed. Scientific research has validated these observations, since BLT has found evidence that the plant stem nodes in crop circles have been exposed to a heat-producing energy, most likely microwaves. The moisture and nutrients which sustain the plant are carried up through the hollow plant stem. This moisture is more abundant at the plant stem nodes. In crop circle plants, massively stretched or elongated apical nodes (the first node beneath the seed-head) are regularly found, as are expulsion cavities (holes blown out at the nodes, usually the lower nodes on the plant stem). Both effects are thought to be the result of the plant stems' internal moisture being exposed to very brief bursts of intense heat, which turns this moisture to steam. The steam then escapes from the uppermost nodes (the youngest and therefore most elastic tissues) by stretching the nodes. Control studies carried out by BLT clearly reveal that mechanical flattening of the plants does not cause these plant stem changes (BLT Research (1)).

Several years ago the BLT team argued that a well-known law of physics, the Beer-

Lambert Principle , which describes the absorption of electromagnetic energy by matter, could be applied to some crop circle cases. Measuring apical node elongation (the stretching of the first stem node beneath the seed-head), it was found that the degree of lengthening decreased as a function of distance away from the centre of a circular formation, and further, that this decrease in node length was logarithmic, thus being in agreement with the degree of change predicted by the Beer-Lambert principle. In another case they presented data showing that the Beer-Lambert principle again applied, but this time in the standing control crop outside the formation. In this case the apical node-length was greatest in the standing crop at the perimeter of the circle, but decreased logarithmically as they sampled farther and farther away from the formation out into the field of standing plants.

The BLT Research Team has reported other interesting findings which support the theory that heat is one of the energies involved in the creation of crop circles. A substantial grant from Laurance Rockefeller in 1999 enabled BLT to commission an X-ray diffraction study on clay minerals taken from a crop circle in Edmonton, Canada. The tests were carried out by material scientist and mineralogist Dr. Sampath Iyengar, who examined specific heat-sensitive clay minerals in these soils. Using X-ray diffraction and a scanning electron microscope, he documented increased crystallization of the clay particles (illite/smectites) in samples taken from within the crop circles as compared to their controls, taken from outside. Statistician Ravi Raghavan confirmed that the increase, although small, was statistically significant. "I was shocked," says Iyengar, a specialist in clay mineralogy with 30 years of experience. "These changes are normally found in sediments buried for thousands and thousands of years under rocks, affected by heat and pressure, and not in surface soils" (BLT Research (2)).

MAGNETIC FIELDS

Another discovery by the BLT Team which indicates the presence of a heating agency also demonstrates the presence of strong magnetic fields when formations are created. Since 1993, when routine soil sampling at crop circle sites was instituted, hundreds of tiny, 10-50 micron diameter magnetized and spherical particles of pure iron have been found in soil samples taken from crop circles. Frequently these tiny iron particles are found clustered along the edges of geometrically circular formations. The fact that these microscopic iron spherules are magnetic means that they were formed in a magnetic field. Their spherical

Facing page, top: Elongated nodes in corn samples from inside a crop circle (Copyright: BLT Research)
Centre: Exploded nodes in corn samples from inside a crop circle (Copyright: BLT Research)
Bottom: Normal nodes in control samples taken outside a crop circle in the same field (Copyright: BLT Research)

Magnetized balls of iron from soil samples from inside a crop circle (Copyright: BLT Research)

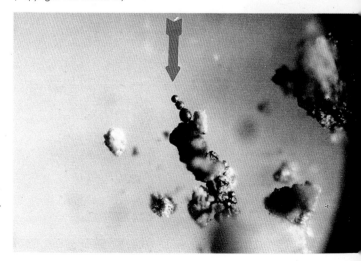

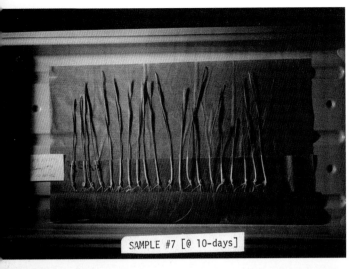

SAMPLE #7 [@ 10-days]

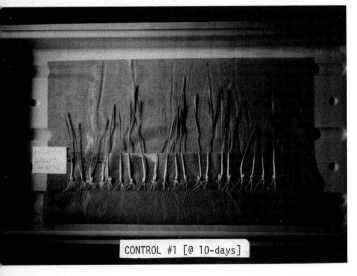

CONTROL #1 [@ 10-days]

Top: Increased growth rates in corn samples taken from inside a crop circle (Copyright: BLT Research)
Above: Normal growth rates in corn samples taken from outside a crop circle, in the same field (Copyright: BLT Research)

shape indicates they were formed as they descended to the earth's surface in a molten state, a situation requiring the presence of temperatures over 1500°C (BLT Research (3)).

ELECTRIC PULSES

The BLT Team has also reported the presence of highly unusual electrical pulses in the crop circle formation process. When crop circles form in mature plants in which the seeds are both present and fully formed, BLT found that these seeds, when germinated, showed enhanced growth rates, sometimes a 4-5 fold increase. Not only did these seedlings grow at an accelerated rate, more significantly they produced greater yield than the controls—and did so even when deprived of water and/or sunlight for long periods of time.

Levengood and Burke were, after years of trial and error, able to replicate the precise intensity level and time-period electrical pulses required by a wide variety of seed, to increase their growth-rate and yield. Thus mimicking precisely the results obtained from the crop circle research, and clearly indicating the presence of these unusual electrical pulses in the crop circle formation process.

When crop circles occur in young, relatively immature plants, however, the seed is quite negatively affected. When these seeds are germinated they sometimes fail to produce seedlings at all. That was what happened with samples taken from the crop circle at Yatesbury in June 2009 (see picture on p.136).

CONTROL STUDIES

The BLT Research Team has also carried out several control studies, in which they have flattened plants by the various methods claimed to have been used by hoaxers, and then sampled and evaluated the plants and soils in their laboratory with their standard testing methods. The results from these control studies have been compared to the results obtained from plants and soils from crop circles in eight different countries over a 12-year period. None of the plant or soil changes outlined above were found in any of the BLT-run control studies, ruling out mechanical or manual flattening of plants as an explanation for the genuine crop circle phenomenon.

BLT'S THEORIES ABOUT HOW CROP CIRCLES ARE FORMED

Since approximately 90% of BLT's test samples of plants and soils from crop circles which occurred during the 1990s in multiple countries show the abnormalities described above—and since these abnormalities are NOT found in the control studies—it is highly likely these changes are indicative of the genuine crop circles. William Levengood suspects that discharging plasma vortices are involved in crop circle formation. Plasma is ionised air, or more simply electrically charged air (read more about plasma vortexes in chapter 4).

Levengood suggests the following hypotheses to explain the anomalous results he has documented in crop circle samples:

In the crop circle which appeared at Milk Hill, Wiltshire, 13th June 2009, the apical nodes were elongated in the areas of flattened crop (Photo: Roy Leraand)

- plasma vortices are forming (for as-yet-unexplained reasons) in the ionosphere and are then spiralling toward the earth along the planet's magnetic field lines, creating crop circles when they impact the earth's surface
- spiraling plasma systems are known to emit microwave radiation, and are also associated with strong magnetic fields and highly unusual electrical pulses
- the microwave component of the discharging plasma system as it impacts the earth's surface is responsible for producing the elongated apical nodes and expulsion cavities
- the unusual electrical pulses also associated with spiralling plasmas are now known to be responsible for the increased growth-rate and yield documented in seedlings grown from crop circles which have occurred late in their growth stage
- because of the strong magnetic fields also associated with spiralling plasma vortices, microscopic particles of meteoric dust in the upper atmosphere are drawn into the descending plasma systems and are then heated to a molten state by the microwaves also present, thus forming molten spheres as they fall through the atmosphere toward the earth
- these tiny magnetized iron spheres are often distributed around the edges of circular components in crop circles, indicating a rotating delivery system consistent with a discharging plasma vortex. (BLT Research (4))

MINISTRY OF AGRICULTURE STUDIES

In 1995, after BLT had published its first results, crop circle researcher Jim Lyons suggested to the Agricultural Development and Advisory Service (ADAS), a section of the English Ministry of Agriculture, that they might test levels of soil nitrogen in crop circles. The project got under way and samples of soil were taken from inside crop circles and from the same fields outside the formations. The samples were analysed at the ADAS laboratories in Cambridge and Wolverhampton, where they found increased levels of nitrates in several of the samples from within the formations.

This is interesting because it has been proposed that nitrates can be formed as a result of natural processes when lightning strikes. The massive energy of a lightning bolt, itself a form of plasma, is sufficient to split oxygen and nitrogen in the air into its constituent atoms, which then recombine to form nitric oxide. Some of this highly reactive gas recombines immediately with oxygen to form nitrogen dioxide, Could there be a connection here to possible plasma mechanisms for crop circle formation?

In most of the tests, an increase of between 30% and 350% was found in crop circle soil nitrate levels compared with surrounding soils. Two of the sets of samples submitted for analysis were from man-made formations, unknown to the testers, and for these the nitrate levels were found to be within the normal range.

Unfortunately these promising research results were not confirmed by further research in subsequent years. Immediately after the study was published, the research department at the Cambridge laboratory was closed down and the project leader himself was made redundant (Anderhub and Müller 2005).

DR. HASELHOFF'S STUDIES

In 2001 the Dutch physicist Dr. Eltjo Haselhoff hypothesised that some crop circles could be made by a small concentrated source of electromagnetic radiation positioned above the field. Utilizing BLT's plant results and their hypothesis that the Beer-Lambert Principle could be applied to their discovery of a linear distribution of elongated apical nodes within a few of the crop circles they worked on, Haselhoff argues that the application of the Beer Lambert principle is not valid. He believes that the absorption of radiation by the air would be insignificant on such a small scale and, also, that the Beer-Lambert Principle assumes a plane source of radiation.

Instead he proposes a point source of radiation, stating that the BLT data fit this model perfectly, thus supporting the idea that such a "point" source (for example in the form of a small ball of light) could be involved in the process of crop circle formation. Haselhoff has also conducted some control work, measusring apical node lengths in a mechanically made (hoaxed) circle and was able to confirm that there was no apical node-length distribution pattern as has been clearly documented in 'genuine' formations. Haselhoff's research was published in the "Letters to the Editor" section of the journal *Physiologia Plantarum*, as a commentary on Levengood & Talbott's earlier peer-reviewed paper published in the same journal in 1999 (Haselhoff 2001).

AMATEUR STUDIES

Of course it's not only scientists who have also tried to throw light on the crop circle mystery. A number of amateur enthusiasts have run their own experiments and projects and have come up with theories about how crop circles are formed and what effects they have on people, animals and electronic equipment.

PLASMA VORTICES AND SOUNDS

In chapter 4 we encountered Terence Meaden's concept of plasma vortices, which he imagined being produced meteorologically by natural whirlwinds spinning so fast that they gained an electric charge. His hypothesis was that these vortices collapsed when they hit the ground, thus pressing the corn down and making crop circles. Levengood, partly building on Meaden's ideas, suggests that plasma vortices rather form in the upper atmosphere before being drawn to earth, and that they give off both light and microwave radiation which soften the plant tissue at the moment of flattening.

Still one of the difficulties with these theories, and the reason why Meaden later rejected them, is that it's hard to see how a whirlwind, with or without plasma, could produce anything other than simple circles.

Meaden did however maintain that plasma vortices can emit both light and sounds. Many eyewitnesses also talk of strange sounds being heard when circles form. Perhaps this may give us a clue as to how plasma whirlwinds might create complex patterns?

The kind of sounds which have been reported from crop circles have been described in various ways: as 'a piercing buzzing', 'like the sounds of static electricity', 'like something between a grasshopper and the buzzing from a high voltage cable' or 'like insect noise, only more mechanical'. Such sounds have been reported both

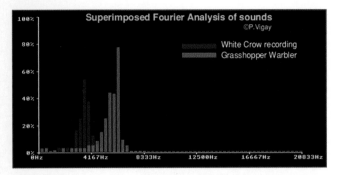

Paul Vigay's analysis of Colin Andrews' sound recording from Hampshire in 1989. Vigay compared the sound in the recording with the song of a grasshopper warbler (a common European songbird). The analysis shows that the sounds are very similar but occupy a different frequency range (centred around 6 kHz instead of 3.5 kHz). Hear the sound recording and read more at www.cropcircleresearch.com/articles/whitecrow.html
(Copyright: Paul Vigay)

from new circles and ones several days old. 'Crackling', 'trilling' and 'hissing' are also words which are often used.

Colin Andrews was the first to report strange sounds from a crop circle. In the summer of 1987 he returned to a crop circle he had already investigated, in order to take further measurements. When he was finished, he got a sudden urge he could not resist:

I turned west, where Stonehenge stood silent, (...) and prayed: "Please God, give me a clue as to what is happening here and help me understand what this is all about". At the precise moment my prayer ended, the exact second, I heard an odd crackling sound from approximately seven or eight feet in front of me that sounded a bit like static, but with a metallic edge to it. It was an unusual, continuous whirring sound at close to ground level and I immediately thought it was being made by some kind of insect. I rejected that straight away because the sound was too mechanical and much too loud for an insect. (...) As the volume of the sound rose, I could feel the air around me begin to move, and I sensed the hairs on my arms standing up and I could feel air pulsating the cheeks of my face. (...) I thought I recognized the sound from my work as an electrical engineer. I had heard similar sounds in laboratories in situations where there was a build-up of high levels of voltage between an anode and a cathode. Just before there is a discharge of electricity, there is an electric purring sound, and that was similar to what I heard in the field (Andrews 2003).

Colin Andrews heard similar sounds in crop circles on several later occasions, and even managed to record them on tape, for example in a 1989 crop circle. The frequency range of the sounds he recorded was between 4 and 6 kHz (Andrews 2003).

Other visitors to crop circles have heard similar sounds, including Andrews' former colleague Pat Delgado. We read in chapter 3 about the Tomlinsons, who heard a shrill, whistling sound which reminded them of pan-pipes while a crop circle formed around them. John Wheyleigh, the cameraman behind the famous Oliver's Castle video, told how he was woken by a grasshopper like sound coming from the field below where he was sleeping and where he then filmed a circle appearing (Thomas 2002).

Cymatics is a field of research which can be interesting to consider in this context. Cymatics was pioneered by Swiss medical doctor Hans Jenny, who experimented for years transferring sound vibrations to liquids and powders. Jenny showed how sound waves could be physically manifested in these fluid materials and how they became visible to the naked eye as symmetrical patterns. In water tanks he produced standing waves in precise geometric patterns, similar to ones which are seen in nature, in art and in architecture. The higher the frequencies he used, the more complex the patterns he recorded (Jenny 1974). Not only are some of the cymatic patterns which have been photographed strikingly similar to certain crop circle patterns, some people think that similar processes could be involved in their formation.

The Canadian-based crop circle expert Freddy Silva has explored the possible connections between sounds and crop circles. In his book *Secrets in the Fields*, he collects research results from various countries to shed light on the subject.

In the 1950s, American agricultural scientist George Smith discovered that when he exposed Illinois cornfields to different sound frequencies, the soil got warmer and the plants took on a slightly burnt appearance. In recent times too, people have commented that the soil in crop circles is often drier than in the soil in the rest of the field, even after rainy nights. Nor is it unusual for corn stalks to look slightly burnt at ground level (Silva 2002).

In the 1960s, two Canadian scientists at the University of Ottawa, Mary Measures and Pearl Weinberger, also experimented with the effects of sound on the germination and growth of spring wheat grains and seedlings. They succeeded in dramatically increasing growth rates of one variety of wheat plants by exposing them to sound frequencies of 5 kHz (Measures and Weinberger 1968).

In 1968 lab experiments at Temple Buell College in Colorado, plants which were exposed to different tones became permanently bent. Plants which were exposed to heavy metal bent away from the loudspeakers or died, while with classical music the plants leant towards the loudspeakers. Exposed to Indian religious sitar music, the plants bent at right angles, like the plants one find in many crop circles (Tompkins and Bird 1973).

'Ultrasound' refers to sounds of any frequency too high for us to hear. It can be aimed and controlled almost like a light beam, and specific frequencies can be focused to cause certain kinds of molecules to vibrate while others nearby are left unaffected. This requires frequencies in the megahertz range, and the higher the

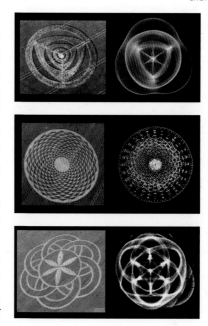

Top: crop circle at East Kennet June 2001, cymatic pattern
Centre: crop circle at Woodborough Hill August 2000, cymatic pattern
Bottom: crop circle at Patcham, East Sussex 2003, cymatic pattern

Geological map of crop circle locations in the mid-1990s

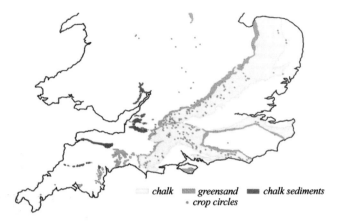

chalk   greensand   chalk sediments
· crop circles

frequencies, the more precise the effects. Silva points out that Levengood's proposed microwaves would kill the corn plants, whereas as we know they continue to live and grow after the crop circles are formed. He suggests instead that ultrasound could be the agency which lays the corn down. In this case, the greater complexity of later crop circles might have required higher frequencies of ultrasound. Silva draws a parallel with the way higher sound frequencies can bring about more complex patterns in cymatics (Silva 2002).

Silva also looks into low frequency sounds, in the infrasonic range. He describes experiments carried out at the Princeton laboratory for Engineering Anomalies Research (PEAR) in the 1980s which used the acoustic power of infrasound to boil water contained under pressure in a hollow cavity. The process can produce local temperatures of hundreds of thousands of degrees for minute fractions of a second. Levengood's theory is that the holes which are found in nodes in corn stalks from crop circles arise when the moisture in the nodes is zapped with a high temperature for a short duration, such as from a microwave source. The moisture turns to steam and the pressure bursts holes in the cell walls of the nodes so it can be released. He also suggests that the sudden powerful heating softens the corn stalk, which being heaviest at the top, collapses under its own weight. Silva proposes that instead of microwaves it could be a combination of infrasound and high pressure which creates the same effects. He further maintains that the vaporizing of water could explain why the earth in crop circles is often dried out (Silva 2002).

Several witnesses have described mist or steam rising from freshly made crop circles. The analysis of the 1996 Oliver's Castle video made by Mike Farrell (London-based expert in technical film analysis) suggested that mist was rising over the central circle as the corn was laid down.

CHALK SEDIMENTS AND GROUND WATER

During the mid-1990s two British researchers, Glenn Broughton and Steve Page, began exploring the idea that geology could be the reason why most English crop circles appear in the same areas every year. By plotting crop circle occurrence on a geological map of southern England, they were able to demonstrate that an overwhelming majority of British crop circles during the years 1993-98 occurred over aquifers lying beneath deep deposits of either chalk or greensand (Sacred Britain Tours). Chalk is a highly porous rock and BLT's John Burke suspected that the spring rainwater percolating slowly down through the chalk over the summer months might increase the ground electrical charge in these areas as the summer progressed. He further speculated that this increase in ground electrical charge might be enough to function as an attractor to the plasma vortices hypothesized by William Levengood as the causative agency behind crop circles - and, further, that this would be particularly evident along the edges of the chalk layers, where the surface water has farther to travel to reach the underground aquifer.

BLT accordingly set out to measure ground electrical charge in the crop circle areas. Readings taken over several summers in the 1990s confirmed that the charge increased during the summer months as the ground dried out (BLT Research (5)). When Burke examined a graph of water-table levels in the Wiltshire area for the years during which crop circles had been reported, he discovered another interesting fact: in two particular years, the water companies had begun to pump the aquifer during the summer months, and it was during those two years (when the aquifer was at its lowest point) that the greatest number of crop circles had been reported.

Andy Thomas has pointed out that there is another factor which could affect the amount of charge created at the ground surface, namely the amount of precipitation seeping through the rock below. If there is a dry spring and summer, hardly any electrical charge may build up. In 2006 there were remarkably few crop circles reported in England - only 46 compared with over 150 in the best years. And the second and third quarters of that year were the driest since 1976. Perhaps insufficient electrical charge in the ground might be a reason for the low numbers of crop formations.

ELECTRONIC EQUIPMENT MALFUNCTIONING

It's not unusual for visitors to crop circles to discover that their electronic equipment starts to behave strangely or that it packs up altogether. Problems with batteries seem to be especially common. Crop circle researcher and photographer Lucy Pringle has been collecting stories of such incidents for many years. The samples below are taken from her book, *Crop Circles, the greatest Mystery of Modern Times.*

Paul Vigay was one of the first to experience mobile telephone failure in a crop circle. As he walked around a crop circle at Alton Barnes in 1991, his mobile stopped working, but as soon as he held it an arm's length outside the formation, he obtained full signal strength. This happened each time he repeated the experiment.

Photographer A.J. Samuels tells how his video camera failed several times when he was visiting crop circles. When he was at the Ogbourne St.George formation in 1992, his newly charged battery, which normally lasted 30 minutes, went flat after only 5 minutes. Something similar happened to him in the Lockeridge circle he visited the same year (Thomas 2002).

In 1995 the well known crop circle photographer Steve Alexander visited a circle at Telegraph Hill. When he entered the formation he laid his second camera (a Nikon) on the ground whilst he assembled his camera pole and took several high shots of the formation, using another camera. When he finished and picked up the Nikon, loaded with fresh V6 batteries, he saw that the light meter glowed very dimly a few times before fading completely. Fortunately he had brought spare batteries, so he swapped them. In the evening when he returned home, he tested the defunct batteries and was surprised to see that they had now come back to life. He found this remarkable, since V6 batteries are not normally rechargeable.

In 1993 Christopher Weeks and a friend of his brought pocket computers into a formation at East Kennet. After leaving the formation both the devices suddenly went dead without any warning. The batteries were completely drained and no warnings came up on the screens to say that they were running low.

I myself have several times experienced sudden battery drain with digital cameras in crop circles. In the summer of 2005 I had with me a brand new Konica Minolta Dimage Z5, which uses four ordinary AA 1.5 volt batteries. A camera which uses ordinary batteries has the advantage that one can buy replacements anywhere so one doesn't have to worry about recharging. No less than three times that summer I encountered a "low battery" warning when I went into a crop circle, despite having replaced the batteries with new ones several times. This happened in the following formations: Winchester on 10th July, East Field on 18th July and Aldbourne on 24th July. I took all these batteries back to Norway with me and tested them with a battery tester. It showed that they were all fully charged.

Tape recorders also have a habit of failing in crop circles. In May 1998 a Wiltshire radio reporter was interviewing a crop circle researcher inside a crop circle, when the tape recorder started speeding up, going faster and faster until it stopped altogether. The researcher had heard of similar cases before and suggested that they move outside the circle. About 45 metres from the formation, the machine worked perfectly again. They repeated the experiment several times, walking in and out of the circle, with the same results. The next day the interview was broadcast complete with the speeded up parts, as the previously sceptical reporter was very impressed with the strange sound effects. Later the same day a TV crew from Western Television was filming in the same circle, and also had trouble with their equipment, which was high quality and had never failed before: the sound turned out to be unusable throughout most of the recording.

EFFECTS ON PEOPLE AND ANIMALS

As mentioned earlier, it's not unusual for people to feel that crop circles affect them on an emotional or spiritual level. People can often experience this just by looking at pictures of crop circles, but stronger effects are common when they physically visit the formations. The typical response is simply intense happiness and physical well-being. Some people sit down to meditate. Others lie down to get the maximum physical contact with the ground inside the circle. Many people only plan a short visit but are later surprised to realize they have been in the circle for hours. Dowsers say that it is especially rewarding to dowse inside a crop circle, as the earth energies are stronger and more focussed there, and people who are especially sensitive to energies can apparently pick up a special crop circle energy in the formation as well.

Visitors to crop circles sometimes talk about prickling feelings in their arms or legs, of waves of heat or cold passing through their bodies, of metallic tastes in the mouth, of headaches or feeling sick. For some people these uncomfortable feelings are so strong that they just have to get out of the formation, or perhaps never go into it in the first place. Most people affected in this way find that the discomfort disappears as soon as they leave the circles, while others may have ill effects which last for several days afterwards.

In contrast to these reactions, some crop circle visitors say they have been cured of pains and ailment by being in the formations. It seems that certain crop circles have had especially strong effects on people, whether in a positive or negative way.

In 1996, two fractal patterns, at Windmill Hill and at Stonehenge, seem to have affected women in particular in strange ways. According to Lucy Pringle, several women who visited the formation reported independently that their menstruation became irregular for several months afterwards. Other women past the menopause suddenly experienced unexpected bleeding (Pringle 1999).

Some people who have visited crop circles have experienced a healing effect just from being inside the formations. In July 1990, Lucy Pringle entered a crop circle at Morestead in Hampshire. She was in considerable discomfort having damaged her shoulder playing tennis the previous evening. As she was sitting down relaxing she became aware of an energy rippling through her shoulder. She gently moved her shoulder and, to her amazement, she found that it didn't hurt any more. She stayed where she was and let the energy flow until her shoulder was completely mobile.

This experience inspired Pringle to experiment in the field of the body's reaction to the crop circle energy. For many years she has measured levels of hormones in people before, during and after visits to crop circles. She reports that levels of thyroxin fall dramatically while her subjects are in the crop circles, while levels of adrenaline and melatonin increase (Pringle 1999).

Not only humans but animals too seem to experience unusual energies inside crop circles. In some cases, Pringle found, dogs have been known to sit down and refuse to go in to the formations. Other times they have followed their owners in, but have showed clear signs of being unhappy, nervous or violent (Pringle 1999).

Perhaps the strangest story about crop circles and animals took place in the summer of 1997. Crop circle researcher Dr. Eltjo Haselhoff had collected corn samples from a circle at Melick in Holland. When he got home, he didn't have time to do anything with them straight away, so he left them in a heap on a table in his garage. There were 15 bunches of about 20 stalks each, some samples from inside the crop circle and some control samples from outside, all clearly labelled. It was several weeks later, when Haselhoff came home from his summer holiday, that he went to sort out the seeds, intending to sprout them and see if there was a difference in germination rates between the corn circle samples and the control samples. Imagine his disappointment when he found that mice had got at the ears of corn, as witnessed by the pile of husks and the droppings left on the floor under the table. The samples were worthless now. But as Haselhoff collected the remains up to throw them out, he noticed something interesting after all. Only the ears from the control samples had been eaten, while the mice had not touched any of the corn taken from inside the crop circle! (Haselhoff 2001).

Facing page: Formation in oilseed rape at Roundway Hill, April 2009
(Photo: Eva-Marie Brekkestø)

CHAPTER 7

WHO OR WHAT IS MAKING THE CROP CIRCLES, AND WHY?

As individuals we have different backgrounds and experiences. So we have different attitudes to the crop circles and are attracted by different aspects of them. An architect or a mathematician might be most intrigued by the patterns and the geometry, while a historian might be drawn to the symbols and a scientist or engineer to the mysterious light phenomena. A biologist or soil scientist might be most interested in research into changes in the soil or the plants, while the aesthetic aspects of crop circles are likely to appeal to an artistic temperament.

In this chapter we shall look at some different approaches to the crop circle phenomenon and will examine various theories about what crop circles are, how they are formed and who or what is responsible for making them.

CONVENTIONAL THEORIES
PEOPLE

Facing page: Ogbourne St.Andrew July 2009
(Photo: Eva-Marie Brekkestø)

The media seem to want us to believe that all crop circles are man-made. Journalists

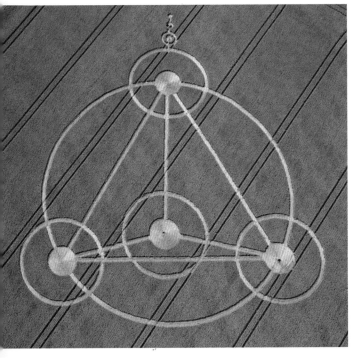

Crop design at Woodborough Hill made by Joachim Koch and team, July 2009 (Photo: Eva-Marie Brekkestø)

rarely have occasion to look into the phenomenon properly. However, those ones who do take the time to study the available facts usually see that the phenomenon cannot entirely by explained by human activities.

Of course there is no doubt that some crop circles are man-made - literally so, it seems, for women are not known to be involved in this activity! In England it's no secret that a few circles are made to order every year, commissioned by TV and film producers or for advertising purposes. In these cases the farmer will be paid for his loss of crop and the circle makers can use as much equipment and take as long as they need (sometimes days rather than hours) to produce a nice accurate pattern. A second type of crop circle is also made with the farmer's permission. In recent years, a group of Germans led by crop circle enthusiast Joachim Koch have made a formation each summer as part of an attempt to communicate with the 'real' circle makers. In July 2009 Koch and his team made the crop circle at Woodborough Hill, for example (see picture on left).

Another category of man-made circle could be called field graffiti. These are usually made at night and in a hurry and can be a messy attempt at some kind of pattern, or just a love-heart with somebody's initials in it. A third category of man-made crop circles are the deliberate hoaxes. Every season, various individuals or groups of people make claims to have made great numbers of crop circles. Often several groups claim to have made the same circle and accuse each other of lying. Of course it would be easy to prove or disprove these claims by publishing photos of the hoaxers in action in a half-finished formation. However, such evidence has never once been forthcoming. Nor have hoaxers ever been caught in the act, despite the intensive observation which all the well-known circle sites are subject to during the season. Hoaxed formations are made at night, and can sometimes be quite complex in design. What characterises them often is that the lay is messy and the corn is heavily flattened to the ground. In other cases the hoaxers can do a neater job, but it is always hard to avoid leaving behind traces of human activity, such as footprints in damp earth, holes where they have used poles for marking out, and 'board marks' or mud on the flattened stems. In fact, even garden rollers and metal bars used to flatten the corn with have been left behind in the fields by clumsy hoaxers! As well as this, hoaxers often fail to get their patterns accurate in the field. Human beings are not perfect and we do tend to make mistakes, especially when working in darkness and under time pressure! Hoaxers measure wrong, stumble in the dark, trample into the standing crop and misunderstand each other. They get interrupted by bad weather and have to make short-cuts. So it's not surprising that the results often don't look very attractive. Incidentally, there is a widespread misunderstanding that if a formation is oval rather than perfectly circular, it must be man-made; but the reverse is actually true. Circles in genuine formations are often not quite circular, sometimes in order to compensate for a sloping field, and also the centre of the swirls is often not in the geometrical centre. On the other hand if a simple circle is drawn by fakers with a rope and a pole in the middle, it can easily be perfectly accurate.

THE MILITARY

It's not unusual to see military helicopters in the air over the English crop circles. This has encouraged some people to believe that the military are somehow making the crop circles, with the help of secret technology, perhaps using lasers and microwaves. Some people even fear that the military makes crop circles to test our physiological and psychological reactions to them and to use that information in psychological warfare. But it's hard to explain with this kind of model how it is that crop circles appear all over the world, and were reported long before the invention of lasers and microwaves.

But the military certainly do follow the crop circles with interest. Visitors to the Wiltshire crop circles can see and photograph military helicopters every single summer. Are they keeping tabs on the circles, or on the people visiting them? Do they know more about the mystery than the crop circle researchers, but are keeping their knowledge secret? Well, there is a much simpler explanation to the military's connection with crop circles. That part of Wiltshire which hosts the greatest density of crop circles is right next to the Salisbury Plain Training Area (SPTA), the biggest military training ground in Britain, and is within a few minutes' flying time of key military installations such as Warminster army base, RAF Lyneham, Middle Wallop Air Army Corps training centre and Boscombe Down experimental testing base. The principal users of the SPTA are in fact the Joint Helicopter Command, so it's not surprising that all kinds of helicopters are constantly seen in the area as they carry out their training exercises and fly to and from the SPTA. And helicopter pilots are only human! Of course when they spot a crop circle, which they can hardly help doing, they are likely to want to take a closer look.

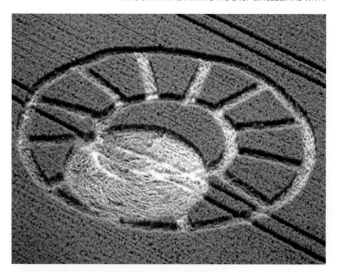

Top: Man-made crop circle at Winterbourne Bassett, Wiltshire June 2008 (Photo: Nick Nicholson)
Above: Close-up of wheat-stalks in the crop circle at Winterbourne Bassett, showing clear marks across the laid corn, caused by a plank or other hard object which has been used to flatten them (Photo: Janet Ossebaard)

Nevertheless it does seem likely that the military would be interested at a command level as well; after all it must seem likely to them that their highly restricted airspace is being trespassed upon on a regular basis by unknown agencies using rather high-tech equipment. The events in Mayville, Wisconsin in 2003 (see chapter 3) also show that the American military, at least, do follow the crop circle phenomenon closely.

A NATURAL PHENOMENON

Might it be that the creator of the crop circles is Nature herself? But how can Nature make something so perfect and beautiful? Well, is a crop circle really more fantastic and incredibly perfect than an ordinary snowflake, for example? And if we had never seen a flower before, surely we would be pretty amazed and impressed the first time we did so.

GOD

If you believe in God, there is no problem explaining crop circles or indeed any other phenomenon. God can produce the most beautiful and mysterious things. And why is God making these fantastic crop circles just now? As a warning maybe? Or perhaps as a means of directing our attention to nature?

THE GAIA THEORY

James Lovelock's Gaia hypothesis describes our Earth as a living, self-regulating organism. Like any living organism, Gaia protects herself and seeks to adapt to the various stress factors she is exposed to, whether these are caused by human activities or other external factors such as meteor strikes or increased solar activity. Perhaps the crop circles could be part of Gaia's self-healing mechanism, working like a kind of acupuncture? Maybe so many crop circles appear in Southern England because the Earth has a large number of acupuncture points in that region? Or, maybe Gaia is making crop circles in order to wake humanity up. The crop circle mystery might perhaps get us to begin to think differently, to develop and to begin to live in harmony with the earth instead of destroying it.

EXTRA-TERRESTRIALS

'Natural' explanations of crop circle formation involving whirlwinds or descending plasma vortices fail to explain how the patterns can be so beautiful and can contain such advanced symbolism and mathematics. For that we need other theories. In chapter 4, I referred to the hypothesis that crop circles are made by intelligent beings from some other part of the universe. One theory is that these ETs visit us in their spaceships and make the crop circles, for example by using phenomena like plasma whirlwinds. Others think that the balls of light which are often observed in and around crop circles could be probes sent out from the spaceships. Most eye witness reports fail to support the idea that ETs make crop circles by physically visiting the Earth. But some do, such as the strange happenings in Poland in 2000 and 2003, described in chapter 4.

Another and perhaps equally popular variant of the ET theory says that the crop circles are made by other civilisations in the universe without them visiting us physically. Adherents of this theory envisage some kind of cross-universe communication through time and space, with us human beings picking up this communication on an unconscious level.

Theories about ETs being responsible for making crop circles got a boost from two remarkable formations, which appeared at Chilbolton in 2001 and Crabwood in 2002 (both in Hampshire). These were very special in that they contained readable messages. Both communicated not through symbols but through coded binary messages, and both included a representation of a face in the crop circle pattern.

CHILBOLTON

On the morning of the 14th August 2001, a face stared up from the field next to a (meteorological) radar dish at Chilbolton in Hampshire. This was the first time a crop circle had reproduced a recognisable picture (see photo p.165). It was in the form of a rasterized image, the same method used for printing pictures in newspapers. Uniquely, the corn was laid as a bitmap so that on the ground absolutely no pattern was discernible, only rows of clumps of wheat. Three days later the face was joined in the same field by a crop formation which became known as 'the data strip'. This also represented an entirely new type of crop pattern, consisting of a rectangle like the first but with 73 rows of 23 small squares of either standing or laid corn. In other words the pattern was a binary one, usually written as a series of 1s and 0s, and it

Facing page: Chilbolton, August 2001 (Photo: Lucy Pringle)

was interpreted as an answer to another binary message - this one sent out from the Arecibo telescope in Puerto Rico in 1974 as part of the Search for Extra-Terrestrial Intelligence (SETI) project.

CRABWOOD 2002

The second 'alien message' formation appeared at Crabwood near Winchester in Hampshire on 15th August 2002. Again a rectangular box encloses a picture of a face, this time with the almond-shaped eyes, large-domed bald head, small mouth and narrow chin of a classic 'Grey' alien. The execution of this picture was different from Chilbolton but equally impressive and unusual, consisting entirely of solid or broken horizontal lines of varying thicknesses, rather like an analogue TV picture.

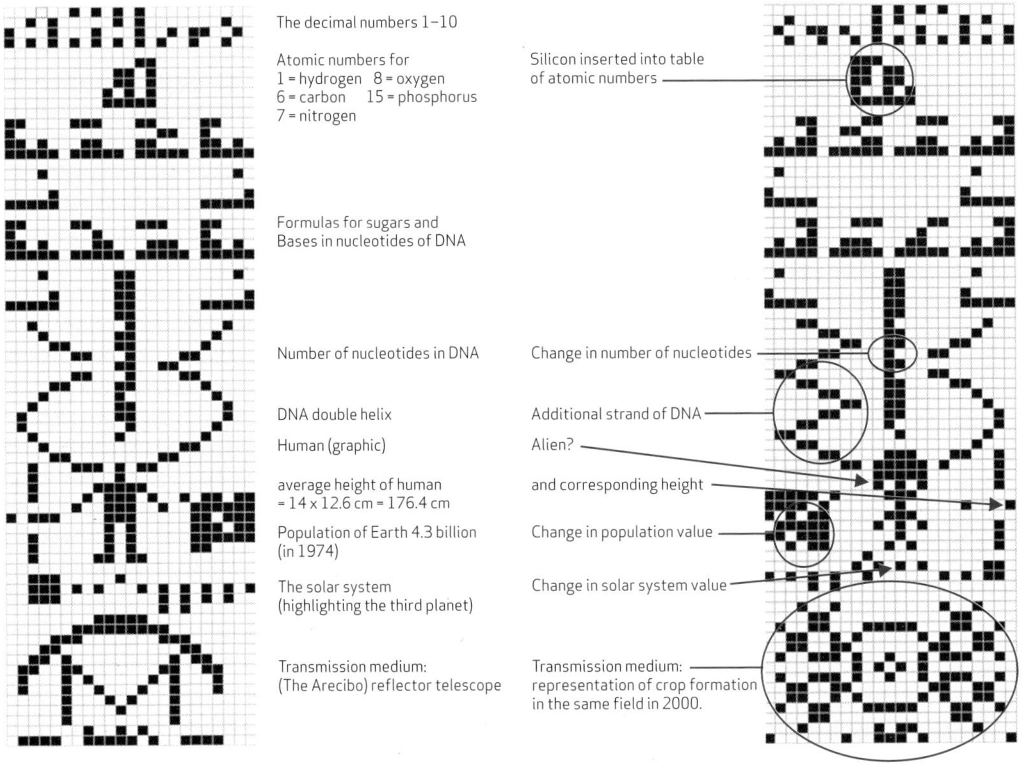

The decimal numbers 1–10

Atomic numbers for
1 = hydrogen   8 = oxygen
6 = carbon   15 = phosphorus
7 = nitrogen

Silicon inserted into table of atomic numbers

Formulas for sugars and Bases in nucleotides of DNA

Number of nucleotides in DNA

Change in number of nucleotides

DNA double helix

Additional strand of DNA

Human (graphic)

Alien?

average height of human = 14 x 12.6 cm = 176.4 cm

and corresponding height

Population of Earth 4.3 billion (in 1974)

Change in population value

The solar system (highlighting the third planet)

Change in solar system value

Transmission medium: (The Arecibo) reflector telescope

Transmission medium: representation of crop formation in the same field in 2000.

Left: Diagram of the message that was sent into space from the Arecibo telescope in Puerto Rico in 1974 as a binary encoded signal. (Illustration: Terje Toftenes)
Right: Diagram of the crop circle at Chilbolton, which can be read as a reply to the Arecibo message (Illustration: Terje Toftenes)

Superimposed on the picture is a circle of laid crop covered in tiny squares of standing corn arranged in a spiral, the whole thing looking from the air a bit like a CD. Once again Paul Vigay was quick to realise that this 'data disc' contained a binary coded message, although very different in format and content from the previous year's message. Paul split up the strings of binary digits on the 'data disc' into groups of eight and took each group to represent a character in the ASCII alphabet, as used in computers. The message which emerged was in English and read as follows : "Beware the bearers of FALSE gifts & their BROKEN PROMISES. Much PAIN but still time. (Damaged word, possibly 'Believe'). There is GOOD out there. We OPpose DECEPTION. Conduit CLOSING (bell sound)".

Many have wondered what the meaning could be behind the non-standard use of small and large letters. Could there be another level of coded message in that as well?

MORE UNCONVENTIONAL THEORIES
OTHER DIMENSIONS AND PARALLEL UNIVERSES

Quantum physicists talk of parallel universes. In each of these there is a copy of ourselves but we have chosen other paths than the one we are on here and now. One version of you is continuing to read this book now. But another one has decided that s/he doesn't want to read any more of it and s/he can't be bothered about these crop circles anymore! This version of you continues in his or her own reality which runs parallel to the reality in which you continue to read this book. This is also how one can explain the paradox of time travel. If you travel back in time and kill your grandmother before your mother is born, a parallel universe splits off in which you and your mother are never born. Physics says that there can be an infinite number of such parallel realities or universes. The idea is that in random quantum processes, the outcome of an interaction is not necessarily 'either/or' but could be 'both/and', if a new universe splits off for each possible result.

When I try to grasp ideas such as this, I think of the book *Conversations with God* by Neale Donald Walsh, which has given me a whole new perspective on existence. In it, 'God' explains that we can live our lives in an infinite number of versions simultaneously. For every choice we make, reality splits up into new versions, and we can live each life as many times as we want or in as many versions as we want,

Facing page: Crabwood, August 2002 (Photo: Andreas Müller)

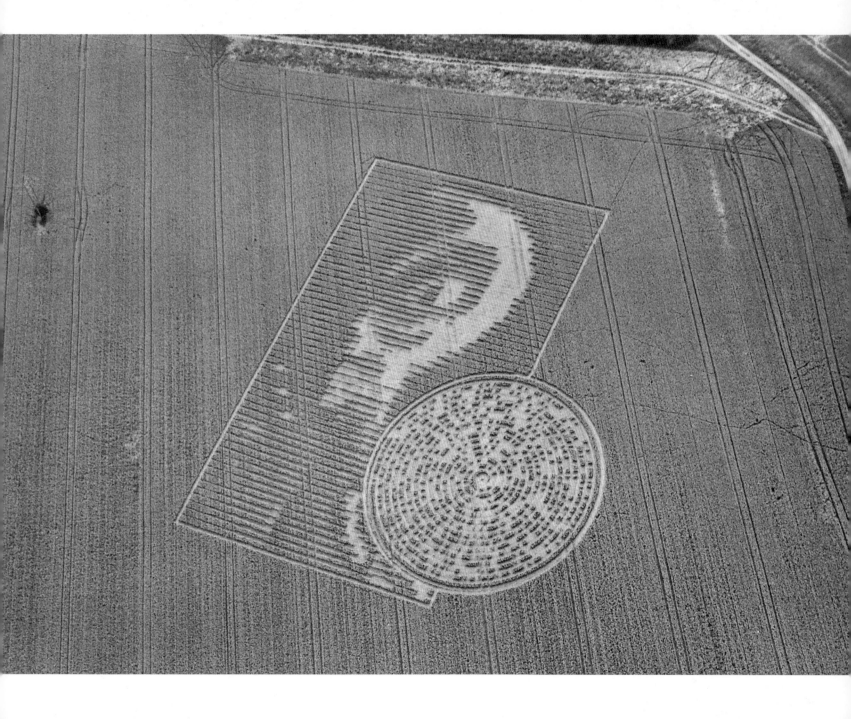

until we have learnt what we wish to learn. The films *Sliding Doors* and *Ground Hog Day* explore the same theme. In Walsh's books, 'God' explains that in the existence we are living in here and now, we have chosen to live with many illusions, including the ideas "we are only living here and now", "time and space are finite and irreversible", and "we are separate from God, from each other and from the rest of the universe". These illusions have the effect that we invest fully in each life and take seriously the 'here and now' choices and challenges.

If we try to look beyond these illusions and imagine that parallel universes really exist, then maybe it is we, in a parallel existence or universe, who are making the crop circles for the other version of ourselves in this existence? Karen Alexander said the following in 2007 in an interview with the Italian website Crop Files:

"Crop circles could be breakthroughs, or incursions from another parallel realm (or realms). I believe UFOs and other paranormal occurrences also work on this level" (Crop Files 2007).

CREATED BY CONSCIOUSNESS

Might the crop circles be generated by the consciousness of the people studying the phenomenon? Freddy Silva has some definite ideas of how that might work. In an interview with the Crop Files website, he answers a question as to the origins of crop circles as follows:

"Hard evidence clearly shows the source is consciousness, and the designs are thought patterns generated by this consciousness. As the 'thought' interacts with our atmosphere and the 3-D world this information splits into what we call light, sound and magnetism, and the effects of such have left appropriate effects on the plants, soil and water. Not to mention human biological fields". And what message is intended by the circle makers? "The awakening of humanity to its responsibility and its higher potential. And the balancing of the Earth, giving us the time to get our act together, because the Earth needs to undergo its periodic shift. They are buying us some time" (Crop Files 2007).

MY PERSONAL JOURNEY

Crop circles change people's lives. Ever since I was captivated by the phenomenon in the mid 90s, it has taken me on an incredible journey. It's important for me to emphasise that the thoughts and conclusions I have come to on this adventure don't constitute any kind of book of answers. Each one of us must sense out which understandings are meaningful for us when it comes to this phenomenon.

When I started out, I was determined to get answers. Who or what was making crop circles, and why? And I thought it was just a matter of time before the world would have a clear answer to those questions.

That answer has kept me waiting, however. Instead, my curiosity to get to the bottom of the crop circle mystery has inspired me to plunge into an array of different subjects I would never have explored otherwise: symbolism, classical philosophy, sacred geometry, mathematics, English history and archaeology, physics, meteorology, music, psychology and so on. The phenomenon has also brought me into contact with many interesting people I never would have met otherwise. In fact I sometimes wonder whether that's not the most important thing about the phenomenon: to bring together people who are curious about the mysteries of life and who think differently from the mainstream.

After I had explored the phenomenon for a few years through reading books and watching DVDs, in conversations and of course in personal visits to crop circles, both in Norway and in England, I felt it was time for me to share my experiences and thoughts with others. I started by giving lectures and as part of that I got in the habit of listing all the possible theories about who was making crop circles: is it our own unconscious minds, is it people in another time or dimension, the Earth itself, extraterrestrials, God? Then one day I realised that it doesn't have to be one answer or the other, it could be all of these agencies together, perhaps in dialogue with each other. It dawned on me that there is no difference between God, the universe, the soul, human consciousness and our planet. Everything is linked, everything is communicating continually and is ultimately one.

The next thing I realised was that this could be the whole point of crop circles. Do they appear precisely in order to make us recognise and experience that unity? Maybe we ourselves, our subconscious and our parallel selves produce the formations in a sort of dialogue with our planet, the universe, God or whatever you want to call the great "all that is". If we can accept that in this way we can participate in creating crop circles, then we have also recognised an entirely new view of existence.

Of course it's much easier to say that 'someone out there' is making them, whether

human beings or extra-terrestrials. Then we can continue to see ourselves as separate from things we don't like, whether 'stupid hoaxers' or 'dangerous aliens' who come to Earth in their big spaceships to invade us. These are basically the two options which the media has chosen to promote.

Numerous apparently serious TV programmes and films have been made which conclude that all crop circles are man-made. Maybe that's not so strange. If you only have a week's time and a limited budget to make a TV programme, you don't really have time to experience and research the phenomenon properly. Moreover, journalists' training is to be critical, and TV companies want to present their viewers with a proper set of answers, not an unsolved mystery. What else can a producer do but track down some hoaxers and pay them to make a circle for the camera?

If you're making feature films, you have another option, of course - you can play the fear and horror cards. Nothing sells like fear! The 2002 film *Signs*, a box-office hit with screen play by M.Night Shyamalan, presents the titillating mystery of 'strange patterns in the cornfields' and gives the explanation in the form of a horror story: the family man and former priest (!) played by Mel Gibson has to battle the devilish little green aliens who have made the crop circles as navigational aids for their planned invasion. He has to fight with both baseball bats and bread knives in order to prevent them conquering the Earth and exterminating mankind.

Even today, after 30 years of regular unexplained crop circle activity, whenever there is any newspaper coverage of a new crop circle, the headlines most often feature the same tired clichés about either little green men from outer space, or students' pranks in the cornfields.

NO ANSWER?

Many people who approach the crop circle mystery imagine they will soon solve the riddle. Some are convinced that an extraterrestrial civilisation is behind it and that this will soon be obvious to everybody. When that doesn't happen some people get frustrated and stop following the mystery while others conclude that the only possible solution is that all crop circles are man-made.

At the beginning of the 20th century, physicists believed they were close to understanding the structure of matter and how the universe works. New laws of physics would soon explain everything. Today it seems that for every new piece of knowledge we gain, we are confronted with an infinite number of new possibilities and questions. From a scientific viewpoint it can thus be said that we are not learning more and more about the universe, but less and less! And not just that: particle physicists have shown that when you go down to the smallest components of the physical world, there is no longer any 'thing' to be examined objectively, since what we can observe changes according to how it is measured, from matter to energy and back again. Ultimately there is no 'real' world out there; we are living in a 'participatory' universe, full of relationships rather than objects.

Perhaps something similar could be said of the crop circles. Perhaps we will get nowhere trying to analyse them objectively? Will we just see more and more detail, like zooming in to a fractal pattern? Is it in fact impossible to be an objective observer of the phenomenon? Do our expectations and our wishes, our hopes and our fears, not simply become an integrated part of the phenomenon itself? In other words, are we helping to create the crop circles and to develop the phenomenon in the direction we want it to go? Are the crop circles just a mirror which is held up to reflect out conscious and unconscious desires?

Perhaps by the time we really get a complete answer to the questions as to who or what is making the crop circles, and why, we will have changed so much as human beings that the questions will seem irrelevant! My conclusion is that crop circles are not a problem to be solved, they are more a mystery to participate in.

CONSCIOUSNESS AND PARTICIPATION

During the first half of 2008, a heated debate raged in the online crop circle forum which I host at www.kornsirkler.no. Sceptics demanded proofs and clear answers, while enthusiasts quickly got told off if they maintained points of view which couldn't be supported by facts. Then, in early August, as the crop circles were gracing the English corn fields with a multitude of beautiful patterns, a contributor sent in the following piece to the forum:

Science is limited, and is not capable of explaining the crucial aspects of our existence. (By science I mean here physics, chemistry and biochemistry, with their established methodologies). (...) This science doesn't explain ethics. Nor art. Nor music. Nor poetry. Nor beauty. Nor human consciousness. Nor religious experience.

Nor mystical experiences. Nor paranormal phenomena. Nor the intrinsic value of nature. Nor what life is. Nor why the world is there. Nor the meaning of existence. And certainly not crop circles. But, since such phenomena and experiences do actually occur, it's clear that we need to look for other ways of understanding than science.

An image: an auditorium full of concert-goers. Some experience the music as a moving and truthful and shaking experience. Others notice little or nothing and go home unaffected. The music played was the same for all, but the listeners have different abilities to hear. Who says that the unaffected ones are right? We need an openness and receptivity in us in order to experience (the music). We almost need faith. (The music) demands a metamorphosis within the listener. But it's NOT a subjective experience, it's an 'intersubjective' one, amongst all of those who are moved. (...) In some way or other, the crop circles relate interactively with the human minds which encounter them. They are probably nearer to humanistic sciences, art appreciation, depth psychology and mystical experience than to the supposedly objective natural sciences. They're not opposed to scientific understanding (as is shown by their geometrical, mathematical, energetic and biological aspects), but they go beyond this understanding and demand alternative approaches as well.

These lines expressed in an astonishingly clear way thoughts I had had myself but had not been able to put into words. I got in touch with the author, who turned out to be Erling E. Guldbrandsen, professor of music studies at the University of Oslo. I found out that he was also the editor or a collection of essays, published as Music and Mystery, and that he had written one of the essays in the book himself. Here he develops the thoughts that he had contributed to the forum:

According to Jung, energy exchange between the unconscious and conscious levels of the psyche is the result of several thousands of years of development. Consciousness is a relatively new phenomenon in the history of mankind. When we dream, when we fall in love, when we suddenly are seized by peculiar impressions, it's not just something we choose. It's something which breaks through, something which happens to us, even if we're reluctant to admit it. We are only partly masters in our own houses. Self-examination and inner work are not very highly valued in the west. But the psyche and the body know better, even if the unconscious layers hardly manage to surface with their mysterious dream images, hunches and intuitions. We are in the possession of an intelligence which is much older than we are ourselves, but which we scarcely recognise.

In the section "The receptivity and tuning of the listener", Guldbrandsen quotes St. Augustine: "One cannot truly understand a phenomenon unless one has first loved it. Receptivity involves the ability to have faith". Guldbrandsen adds: "The extraordinary experience demands participation, almost co-creation in the listening. It demands openness, and almost more than that: an activated capacity, a faculty in me which can meet a revelation, seize it and accept it into my being". (Guldbrandsen and Varkøy 2004).

AN INTERACTIVE PHENOMENON

As soon as one gets involved in the crop circle phenomenon, one gets a feeling that the phenomenon is communicating with its observers, and if one follows it for a period of time, a clear pattern emerges. Even initially sceptical crop circle researchers have found to their surprise that apparently fortuitous coincidences are constantly occurring when it comes to when and how crop circles appear and what the patterns look like. Sometimes one feels like one is taking part in a sort of experiment, a dialogue, a process of two-way learning and self-development. Some people describe a feeling of being observed, that the creative powers behind the phenomenon know their thoughts and feelings, and are in a way including them in the phenomenon. Others get the feeling of being participants in the creative processes themselves.

The strange coincidences that people experience around the crop circles are known as synchronicities. Most crop circle researchers have had several experiences of this type. In some cases, students of the phenomenon wish for particular patterns to form or for circles to form under certain conditions, and they appeal to the creative forces behind the phenomenon to respond. Here are some well known examples of 'prayers' being answered in this way.

On 23rd August 1986, Colin Andrews and Busty Taylor were flying over Cheesefoot Head close to Winchester, Hampshire to photograph two crop circles in a field called The Punch Bowl. As they were leaving the area heading south, Taylor looked at Andrews

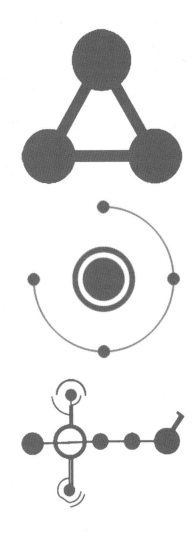

Top: Diagram of the crop circle below Oliver's Castle, July 22nd 1992
Middle: Diagram of the crop circle at Cheesefoot head, August 23rd 1986
Above: Diagram of the crop circle at Charley Knoll, July 14th 1993

Facing page: the Avebury web, August 1994 (Photo: Andrew King)

and said how nice it would be if they were to find a crop circle where all the patterns that they had seen over the years were overlaid into one integral design, forming something like a Celtic cross (Ed.: a quintuplet with the 4 satellites placed on a ring). The very next day, Busty and a fellow researcher by the name of Omar Fowler were flying over that same area. When the aircraft reached the point where Busty had made that remark the day before, they spotted a new crop circle consisting of a large circle surrounded by a ring with four smaller circles each at the cardinal compass points: the design of a Celtic cross (Andrews and Delgado 1989)!

In July 1992, Dr. Steven Greer, the founder and director of the Center for the Study of Extraterrestrial Intelligence (CSETI), was leading a tour party to Wiltshire. ON the 22nd July, he and four other members of the group met at Woodborough Hill in Wiltshire to conduct an experiment. They meditated on a predetermined pattern consisting of three circles arranged in a triangular fashion, each linked by three straight lines. The following morning a report came in of a new formation below Oliver's Castle, which bore an exact likeness to the meditated pattern (Silva 2002).

Inspired by Greer's project, a group of crop circle enthusiasts in the East Midlands decided to carry out their own experiment. During May and June 1993, the group held a series of meditations focusing on a particular design which they intended would form in a certain field near Husbands Bosworth in Leicestershire which had hosted circles in each of the previous 4 years. They would then be waiting at the field and would hope to see the formation appear. On the final meeting before the scheduled crop watch, however, everyone had difficulty concentrating on the image selected. They agreed to a change of plan and instead decided to let the circle makers guide them: then they each drew the images that came into their heads. On the night of the crop watch, 3rd July, various paranormal events took place but no circle appeared. However, on the 7th July at a new location, Charley Knoll, half way between Husbands Bosworth and Belper, where they had sat and meditated, a large and complex formation did appear. The pattern (diagram to the left) consisted of seven circles arranged in a cross, with various corridors, arcs and appendages, and the group was delighted to see that all the elements they had drawn after their final meditation were included. They also noticed that there were seven members in the group, seven main circles in the pattern and that it appeared on the 7th day of the 7th month! (Douglas 2004).

In 1995, the Southern Circular Research Group led by Andy Thomas carried out another experiment. One evening when the group met, one of the members, Barry

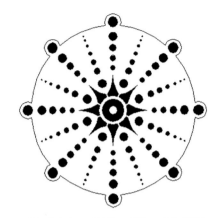

Diagram of 'sun' circle at Old Shaw Village July 2001

Reynolds, expressed a strong sense that a crop formation would appear containing six circular elements. Reynolds drew the formation he had in mind: a circle, another circle surrounded by a ring, and yet another circle surrounded by two rings. Several days later, on 28th June the group held a meditation at Wolstonbury Hill in West Sussex, focusing on Reynolds' drawing. Two days later, on 30th June, the group members were told about the discovery of a new formation at Felbridge, West Sussex. Upon investigation, this formation turned out to be identical to Barry Reynolds's drawing (Bura and Thomas 1997).

Late in the afternoon of 25th July 1995, Andreas Müller and two friends were visiting a new crop circle at Roundway near Devizes in Wiltshire. The formation was placed right under the power lines that ran across the field. Andreas continues: "It had been a long day, it was hot, and we would have liked to just hang out in the crop circle for a while, but the constant electrostatic buzzing from overhead soon drove us out of the field. As we made our way out along the tramlines, one of my companions, Sven Reuss, remarked in passing: "I don't see why, in such a huge cornfield, the crop circles have to be put right under these power cables! If it was up to me where to put them, I'd have chosen that area over there at the foot of the hill!" Around 8 a.m. the next day, the farmer called us again to tell us that a new crop circle had appeared in the same field that morning. When we got there, we remembered with amazement the remarks that had been made the day before. The new formation, an elegant 75 m wide ring with two swirled circles inside it, was placed exactly on the spot which only a few hours earlier Sven had picked out as his preferred place to put a crop circle!" (Anderhub and Müller 2005).

In 1999, a Japanese film crew accompanied by the writer and metaphysics researcher Maki Masao was in Wiltshire to make a television program about crop circles. On 27th July Masao took the group to a formation opposite Silbury Hill. There they carried out a meditation experiment asking for a formation to appear that night, close to Silbury Hill, slightly to the west, and containing a Japanese element. The next morning they learned that a new formation had been discovered at Beckhampton. Only minutes later they flew over the formation. The magnificent pattern had all four features: it was located close to Silbury Hill, a bit to the west, it had appeared that night, and it clearly contained Japanese elements: the pattern looked like origami, and it also represented a common Japanese family crest (Janssen and Ossebaard 2001).

In July 2001, a group of American circle watchers were in Wiltshire with Denni Clarke. On the evening of the 21st July the group sat down to carry out an experiment Everyone in the group drew a sketch of a pattern. Then they put all the sketches together to make one crop circle pattern, consisting of a five-armed star inside a triangle. The triangle had crescent moons along each side and spiral arms of circles coming out of each corner. The group then meditated and asked for the pattern to manifest as a crop circle. Two days later a new circle was found at Silbury Hill. The pattern had several of the wished-for features, consisting of a triangle with a double circle inside and spiral arms of circles coming out of each corner (Anderhub and Müller 2005, p. 72).

In July 2001 a Swiss group led by Werner Anderhub was in Wiltshire to see the crop circles. The day before they left, the 27th July, they meditated together at Avebury Henge in an attempt to contact the unknown intelligence behind the crop circles. They expressed a simple wish that a new crop circle would appear somewhere in the area the next night, and that it should be some kind of a sun symbol. That evening Anderhub drove the group to the airport. But early the next morning he was out on his usual inspection of the fields together with Andreas Müller. At 4:30 a.m. on a slope near Old Shaw Village they spotted a new formation. Climbing the hill opposite for a better view, they soon saw to their astonishment that the pattern was a beautiful sun symbol with 16 'rays' of smaller circles.(Anderhub and Müller 2005, p. 66).

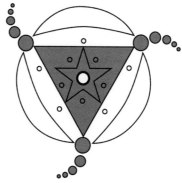

In the summer of 2002, I was in Wiltshire with Guro Parvanova and two other Norwegians. We rented a cottage in Manningford Abbot about three kilometres south-east of the village of Pewsey. From the garden we had a view out to the Pewsey White Horse on Pewsey Hill. Just before midnight on 16th July, Guro was standing outside the house when she caught sight of some lights moving horizontally across the night sky, before going down to the ground somewhere in the east. She called us to come and look. When we got there, there were no lights to see, but we could tell that where the lights had gone down towards the ground must have been between the house and the White Horse. Before we went to bed, we joked that maybe a crop circle would appear there during the course of the night.

Top: Diagram of crop circle near Silbury Hill July 2001
Centre: The pattern Clarke's group meditated on, drawn by Andreas Müller after a sketch by Denni Clarke
Over: Diagram of crop circle at Beckhampton July 1999

The next morning we had forgotten the whole episode and drove off in the opposite direction to the crop circle cafe, then at Cherhill, to hear if there were any reports of new circles in the night. We were met at the door by Francis Mallett, who wondered

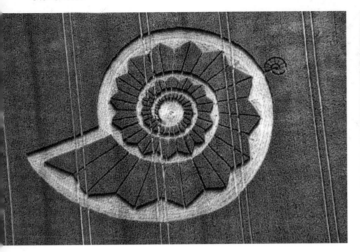

Above: The Nautilus formation at Pewsey, July 2002 (Photo: Andrew King)
Right: The Swastika at Pewsey, 2004 (Photo: Steve Alexander)

why we had come all the way up to Cherhill instead of going to look at the fantastic new crop circle next to the Pewsey White Horse! We jumped back in the car and drove the half hour back to Pewsey. We found the path to the White Horse but were disappointed to discover that the farm manager was quite aggressively denying visitors entrance to the field. We tried to persuade him but without success. Some other crop circle enthusiasts we met advised us to go and ask the landowners instead. We drove the short distance to their house and rang the bell. Out came a friendly lady who introduced herself as Elli Strong. We explained that we had come all the way from Norway to see the crop circles and that we very much wanted to visit just that crop circle because we'd seen these strange lights the night before which might have been involved in making it.

Luckily for us, Mrs Strong had been to Norway and was well disposed to Norwegians. She went and got her husband's agreement, on condition that we came back afterwards and told her what we thought about the circle!

We went off very happily to look around the beautiful formation, which had the shape of a nautilus sea-shell. Afterwards we sat in Elli's garden and told her all about

Windmill Hill 2004 (Photo: Eva-Marie Brekkestø)

the attractive lay and the unusual design. Elli was amazed that the design was of a sea-shell. She had just been making a shell-fish lunch for her and her husband's wedding anniversary and had been standing thinking of their house at the seaside. This was the beginning of a very nice friendship with Elli and James Strong.

Two years later, on 19th July 2004, we invited the Strongs and Charles Mallett to lunch in the house we had rented in Avebury that year. Naturally crop circles were the main topic of conversation, and several times we said how exciting it would be if a new one would appear on their farm that same night. However, we discounted that as unlikely, since the Strongs had already had two formations on their land that summer, and they usually get one each year. James joked that he had better go home and make one for us.

Next morning at 8 a.m., Elli ringed me. Sounding shaken, she said simply: "Eva, it's here. Come at once!" We picked up Charles and drove to Pewsey. Under Pewsey Hill with its White Horse lay a new crop circle. It had an airy, totally pristine lay and was in the shape of a cross with four wavy arms and a circle at the end of each arm.

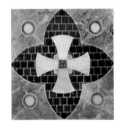

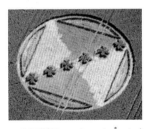

Top: Gulset, Skien, Norway 2007 (Photo: Jostein Åsebø)
Centre: The frieze from the church in Marlborough (Photo: Bert Janssen)
Bottom: Crop circle at Savernake Forest, July 2005 (Photo: Bert Janssen)

Facing page: Upper Upham 1st August 2007 (Photo: Axel Kayser)

On the 16th July 2004, my friend Bente and I went for an afternoon walk from Avebury to Windmill Hill. For the second year running Bente was in Wiltshire to look at crop circles. After we'd turned into the track up towards Windmill Hill and were walking past the first cornfield on the right hand side, Bente pointed out into the field and exclaimed: "Here there's going to be a crop circle soon". When I asked her why she said that, she answered that she just suddenly got a feeling. I replied that she might well be right, as Windmill Hill usually hosted a crop circle most summers and had not done so thus far that year. But I also pointed out that the formations usually appear further up towards the top of the hill and not where she was pointing.

The same evening we met Charles Mallett, who was going to spend the night out crop-watching. However he hadn't decided yet where to go, so I suggested that in view of Bente's sudden inspiration, he should choose Windmill Hill. Charles asked Bente if she was usually clairvoyant, and when she answered in the negative, he decided to spend the night on another hill-top.

Early next morning, Charles phoned. He had just got a call from a friend who had told him about a new crop circle - on Windmill Hill! We hurried there straight away. A gigantic new crop circle was right where Bente had said it would be.

On 1st August 2005 Bert Janssen, Janet Ossebaard and some other Dutch friends gathered for a lively social dinner at the Black Horse pub in Cherhill. They decided to see if together they could manifest a crop circle with a new pattern which hadn't been used before. They chose a photo which Bert had taken earlier in the day of a frieze in a mediaeval church in Marlborough, showing an unusual design of rosette-like cross which they took to be a cross of the Knights Templar. For just a couple of minutes they all focused on the picture and then returned to merrymaking and forgot all about it. Two days later Janet heard about a new formation near to Savernake Forest, east of Marlborough. Janet found a circle containing a square with a diagonal line of six crosses which she was delighted to find bore a resemblance to the central parts of the cross in the photo.

On the 26th June 2007, I got a call from a young man called Erik who lives in Skien in southern Norway. Erik was 19, had just come out of school and had been very engaged with the crop circle mystery for the previous six months. He'd spent a lot of time exploring the phenomenon and during the past months he'd been in frequent correspondence with me by e-mail. He was very taken up with the idea that the circles must be man-made. Erik was critical of BLTs research which he thought was unscientific

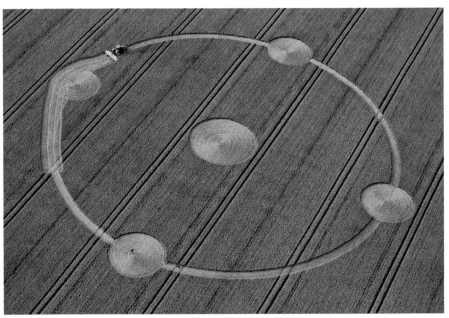

Top: View from Hackpen Hill 31st July 2009 (Photo: JJ, © Radek Kopij)
Right: The crop circle below Hackpen Hill 2009
(Photo: Eva-Marie Brekkestø)

and not rigorous enough. He was also very keen to put this point of view across on the website of the Norwegian Crop Circle Group, first in the guest book and later in the forum.

Erik now told me that he had been on the bus that afternoon on his way home from his summer job. As the bus passed the suburb of Gulset, he caught sight of a crop circle just near the road (see top photo p 180). He got off at the next stop and ran back to the circle, from where he was now ringing me. Immediately I told him that I had a strong feeling this circle was for him. This circle, the first significant one in Norway since 2002, the first reported from Telemark county and the first in the Skien area, had to be a gift for Erik so that he could see the phenomenon in a new light. For despite his negative attitude, he really did very much long to see a crop circle. He was very enthusiastic when he rang me, and I didn't hold back from expressing my feeling about the circle being meant for him. For a while he let himself be carried away by the moment and the incredible synchronicity of his finding the circle. However it didn't take long before he returned to his usual sceptical stance and expressed his belief that this circle too could be man-made.

At the time I was on my way to hold a seminar and couldn't go to see the circle myself but luckily I got hold of Jostein Åsebø who lives in Skien and had been to see crop circles in England before, so had some experience. His report and the clear photographs he took showed a flowing, airy and undamaged lay, which was not in the least reminiscent of the mess which plankers make when they flatten a circle.

Late Thursday evening the 30th of July 2009, Radek Kopij, his son Tymek and his Irish friend J.J. decided to spend the night on Hackpen Hill. They meditated and asked for a crop circle to appear. And it did!!

Radek wrote this testimonial for the Crop Circles Norway website (edited):

My name is Radek Kopij. I am Polish, but I've lived in Dublin for the past five years. I came to England for one week to visit my son Tymek and travel around with my friend JJ. Before I came, JJ had told me about the crop circles phenomenon, but to be honest I didn't give much credit to his story. Things soon changed soon though. We visited a few crop circles and I realised that this was something out of this world. Anyone with common sense who enters a crop circle for the first time can clearly understand that this is something not made by humans.

On Thursday the 30th of July, the three of us sat on Hackpen Hill and meditated for 2 hours. Mentally we sent good wishes and love to the beings creating the circles. We visualised that they answered our call and gave us some sign of their existence. We fell asleep at 2:30 am.

Next morning I woke up, doubting that anything would have taken place. I was thinking that it would have been so nice if a crop circle was somewhere around, but the next moment I was telling myself not to hope so much, to protect myself from being disappointed. To stop this confusion I climbed on the top of JJ's van. What I saw shocked me. In the wheat field right below Hackpen Hill field was a newly made circle. A beautiful and simple 'quintuplet' of five circles.

The three of us ran down the hill past the White Horse and into the centre of the new formation. But at 8.30 am our happiness and excitement were ruined as the farmer turned up with his tractor and mower and set about destroying the pattern. The whole thing was gone in a few minutes. Luckily we had managed to take some pictures of the crop circle while it was intact.

MANIFESTED DREAMS

Ed and Kris Sherwood have an interesting way of looking at the crop circles phenomenon. They say that the messages in crop circles come from a level of consciousness that requires us not only to observe them but to interact with them if we wish to decipher their meaning.

In their own words, *"We're meant to think, we're meant to investigate. We think that the messages are coming from our collective consciousness. They appear to us like dream symbols for things that have been suppressed from our conscious minds, things we haven't been dealing with. They're symbolically trying to draw our attention to these issues, the way poltergeist activity will manifest. It's like a dream, but one which has been conceived by the collective consciousness. The crop circle is made up of more information than our conscious mind. That's why we tend to feel that it's conceived by something greater than ourselves."*

A purely intellectual approach seems to bring us only a short way in our understanding of the crop circle phenomenon. We perhaps need to apply other methods to get deeper into the phenomenon.

In 2005 Allan Brown made a statement which might help us to get back on track when our usual analytical approach becomes too single-minded:

"The best crop circle material comes from those who engage with the phenomenon in an open poetic, imaginative way. As soon as you try to get to the bottom of the phenomenon in any rational, analytic way, you must reach the conclusion that most of the formations are probably man-made, and it is unlikely that you'll ever in any tangible sense work out which are which in any given season. In fact as soon as the notion of who's making them gains the upper hand, the poetic quality of the work will begin to fall away." (Toftenes 2005).

Facing page: Crop circle at Lockeridge, Wiltshire, July 2008
(Photo: Eva-Marie Brekkestø)

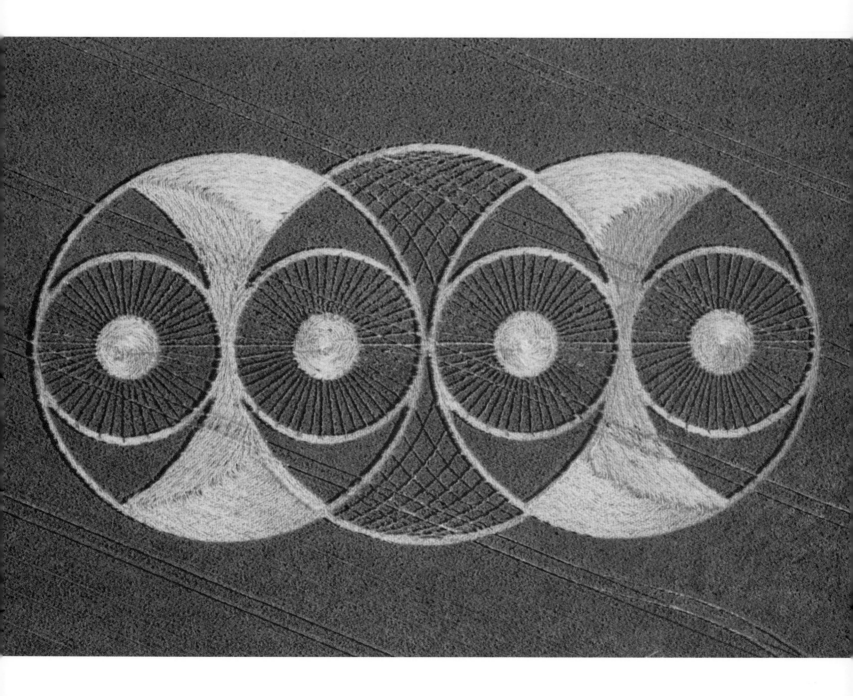

CHAPTER 8

WHAT DO THE CROP CIRCLES MEAN?

SYMBOLS

My own deep fascination with the crop circle mystery began in the mid-1990s, as I mentioned earlier, when I saw a picture of the triangular formation at Barbury Castle in 1991 (see photo on page 9). As I sat looking at this picture, I felt very moved, and decided that I just had to find out more about this phenomenon. Later I learnt from Freddy Silva that the pattern at Barbury Castle may be a representation of an ancient symbol known as the 'Kabbala in Alchymia. Apparently this symbol was seen as very powerful, and shows how our material world is brought to life by a divine spark which moves around the circles in the diagram. When these circles are activated, the creative process can start (Silva 2002). This formation, which was found on the 17th July 1991, also became very famous because it was referred to by many as the first truly complex pictogram. After a while I gathered that Barbury Castle had been the start of a deep interest in the crop circle phenomenon for many others besides me (see picture on p.9).

Up until 1991 most crop circles had consisted of just circles or rings. This formation at Barbury Castle marked the start of a new era in the history of English crop circles, along with the formation which arrived at Ickleton near Cambridge on the 13th August the same year. The formation at Ickleton clearly expressed a mathematical meaning. It depicted an example of a known mathematical figure, called the Mandelbrot set after its discoverer

Facing page: Crop circle at South Field Alton Priors, Wiltshire, July 2008
(Photo: Eva-Marie Brekkestø)

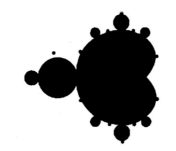

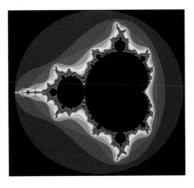

Top: Diagram of Mandelbrot crop circle at Ickleton near Cambridge 1991
Above: the Mandelbrot fractal

Left: Diagram of a 'dumbbell' type crop circle at Furnes, Norway, 2000
Right: Diagram of a 'dumbbell' type crop circle at Syverstad, Norway 1999

Benoit Mandelbrot, who founded the branch of fractal mathematics.

The majority of crop circle patterns fall into three categories:

- resentations of known symbols from different cultures
- patterns derived from nature
- patterns with explicit mathematical or geometrical content

There are patterns which are combinations of these categories, and some that simply seem to be playful displays of geometry and shape. A couple of formations have not fitted any of these categories, like the two 'alien faces' of 2001 and 2002. These contained decipherable messages which seemed to be from extraterrestrial civilisations.

KNOWN SYMBOLS

As early as the 1980s, some of the first of the more complex circles in England were recognised as existing symbols. For example some people have said that the so-called dumb-bell patterns, two circles joined by a straight line, symbolise 'contact between heaven and earth' in an Indian tradition.

Throughout the 1990s, one pattern which was very common was the quintuplet, consisting of four small circles positioned around a larger central circle. Sometimes the satellites were placed on a ring as well, in which case some authors have referred to them as 'Celtic crosses', and these were still turning up ten years later as an element in more complex designs; for example, at Everleigh Ashes in Wiltshire in 2000 there appeared a special variant, in which the central circle consisted not of laid crop but of a Neolithic tumulus, on which the whole formation was centred. In this case the grass and wild plants growing on the mound were also flattened and swirled (see picture on p.190).

Many other symbols from many different cultures have been reproduced as crop circles. Here are some well known examples:

- September 1993, Bythorn, Huntingdonshire: Indian mandala
- 6th May 1997, Barbury Castle, Wiltshire: The Tree of Life in the Kabbala (in flowering oil-seed rape)

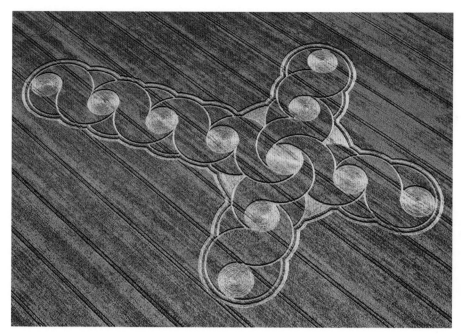

Top left: Etchilhampton Hill 2008 (Photo: Axel Kayser)
Top right: Highclere 2002 (Photo: Lucy Pringle)
Above: Grey Wethers 2009 (Photo: Eva-Marie Brekkestø

- 4th May 1998, Silbury Hill, Wiltshire: the Celtic sun-wheel or 'Beltane Wheel'
- 20th June 1999, Silbury Hill, Wiltshire: the Egyptian symbol 'Horus' wings'
- 28th July 1999, Beckhampton, Wiltshire: Japanese family crest
- 3rd June 2001, Wakerly Woods, Northamptonshire: Mayan calendar
- 21st July 2002, Highclere, Hampshire: the pyramid and the eye (Egyptian and Freemason)
- 15th July 2002, Adam's Grave, Wiltshire: Yggdrasil, the world-tree
- 9th August 2005, Marden, Wiltshire: Maya symbol
- 14th July 2009, Grey Wethers, Wiltshire: yin-yang symbol
- 15th July 2008, Etchilhampton Hill, Wiltshire: Celtic Cross

The fact that the patterns use symbols from many different cultures perhaps tells us that the crop circles are not intended to address just one particular ethnic or cultural group. They might be communicating that no one religion has a monopoly of the truth, and that we can only achieve a deeper understanding of existence and the

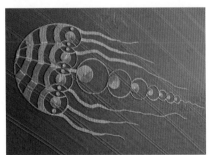

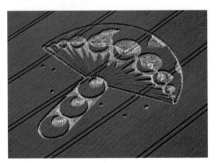

Top: Crop circle at Everleigh Ashes 2000 (Photo: Andreas Müller)
Centre: Wayland's Smithy 2009 (Photo: Roy Leraand)
Bottom: Rough Hill 2009 (Photo: Eva-Marie Brekkestø)
Facing page: Beacon Hill 2004 (Photo: Steve Alexander)

universe when all religions can see beyond their own limited points of view and can join together to seek a common understanding of mankind and the universe.

PATTERNS FROM NATURE

Many crop circle designs through the years have incorporated elements which resemble animals, parts of plants, physiological, physical or astronomical features. Here are some fine examples:

- 10th August 1994, Avebury, Wiltshire: spider's web
- 26th June 1995, Cheesefoot Head, Hampshire: the inner planets of the solar system
- 14th July 1997, Henwood, Hampshire: ant
- 3rd May 1999, Wallop, Hampshire: stages of a solar eclipse
- 25th July 2001, Gog Magog Hills, Cambridgeshire: angel
- 28th August 2002, Crooked Soley: DNA spiral (photo p. 201)
- 10th August 2003, North Down, Wiltshire: a molecule
- 26th June 2004, Milk Hill: bee
- 28th July 2004, Beacon Hill, Berkshire: dolphins (photo p. 191)
- 21th August 2005, East Field, Wiltshire: scarab beetle
- 16th July 2007, Hailey Wood, Wiltshire: butterfly (photo p.192)
- 23th July 2008, South Field, Wiltshire: swallows (photo p. 187)
- 3rd June 2009, Yatesbury, Wiltshire: dragonfly
- 29th May 2009 Wayland's Smithy, Oxfordshire: jellyfish (photo p. 190)
- 24th June 2009 Rough Hill, Wiltshire: mushroom (photo p. 190)
- 2nd July 2009, Stanton St. Bernard, Wiltshire: humming bird

PATTERNS WITH EXPLICIT MATHEMATICAL OR GEOMETRICAL CONTENT

Many crop circle patterns fall into this category. Often categories 1 and 2 also include mathematical elements. Here are some of the famous formations in this category:

- 13th August 1991, Ickleton, Cambridgeshire: Mandelbrot set (photo p.188)
- 7th July 1996, Stonehenge, Wiltshire: Julia set fractal

Above: Hailey Wood 2007 (Photo: Eva-Marie Brekkestø)
Facing page: Chute Causeway 2007 (Photo: Axel Kayser)

- 29th July 1996, Windmill Hill, Wiltshire: triple Julia set
- 11th July 1997, Alton Barnes, Wiltshire: a torus knot (photo p.205)
- 8th August 1997, Milk Hill, Wiltshire: fractal of triangles
- 24th July 1999, Silbury Hill, Wiltshire: fractal based on triangles and squares
- 28th July 2001, Cliffords Hill, Wiltshire: fractal based on circles (photo p. 194)
- 13th August 2001, Milk Hill, Wiltshire: six fold Julia set (photo page 194)
- 20th July 2006, Straight Soley: representation of a four dimensional torus (photo p. 203)
- 26th July 2007, Chute Causeway, Wiltshire: fractal pattern based on pentagons and pentagrams (photo p.193)
- 1st July 2008, Barbury Castle, Wiltshire: demonstration of the number Pi (photo p. 207)

WHAT ARE SYMBOLS?

Many people have seen crop circle patterns as a form of coded message which we are supposed to decode and understand intellectually. Some have tried to categorise the patterns to see if they could crack the code. But nobody has really succeeded, apart from understanding the messages hidden in the 'mathematical' patterns.

Most crop circles are written in symbolic language, not as codes to be deciphered. Symbols of this kind are complex and subtle and can't be pinned down to one specific meaning. Instead they represent the sum of all the meanings we can associate with them. Therefore we cannot define the exact meaning of a crop circle symbol, only say what meaning it might have in one context or for each one of us. Why do crop circles contain such ambiguous symbols? Many people ask themselves why, if crop circles come from an intelligent source, they cannot give clear messages in a known language, such as English? One answer might be that as long as crop circles are ambiguous, they don't exclude anyone, but speak in principle to everyone. In our western culture we seek for precise meanings. We are analytical and want clear answers. Perhaps we can't get those kinds of clear answers when it comes to crop circles? Or maybe we should be asking different kinds of questions?

Language speaks above all to the intellect, whereas symbols also affect us on another level, that of the unconscious and the emotional. When a new crop circle appears, the aerial photos set off a process of associations in people who follow them. If you visit the

Above: Cliffords Hill 2001 (Photo: Janet Ossebaard)
Right: Milk Hill 2001 (Photo: Janet Ossebaard)

Crop Circle Connector website during the summer season, you can see how different people bring their own ideas and associations to the analysis of each formation. A stimulating exchange of opinions often results when contributors bring in their understanding of other symbols, their mathematical knowledge and their artistic appreciation. In this way, symbols which are in themselves ambiguous trigger a process of exploration of their possible meanings, leading eventually to a deeper understanding.

Sometimes we cannot find articulate meanings in the patterns and have to let them speak to them on a more subconscious level. I am not alone in believing that the symbols could be designed to press buttons and to set processes going in us, as I mentioned in chapter 7. Everybody who studies crop circles falls for certain individual patterns which s/he thinks are especially beautiful or exciting. Maybe it's just these patterns which can trigger processes of change in that person.

MATHEMATICS AND MUSIC

"The cosmos was formed according to and upon the basis of laws which are expressed as music, arithmetic and geometry, they bring about order, harmony and balance." Edgar Cayce

SACRED GEOMETRY

The mathematicians, architects and artists of classical antiquity were preoccupied by considerations of form. They understood that the geometrical proportions of buildings or artworks strongly affect how they are experienced by people, and took care in combining numbers, shapes and proportions in order to create a special ambience. The master designers of the Gothic cathedrals revived this ancient knowledge, which is now referred to as 'sacred geometry'. Among the most prevalent traditional geometric forms ascribed to sacred geometry are the sine wave, the sphere, the vesica piscis [8] the torus and the Golden Mean.

We only need to enter a mediaeval cathedral to experience that the builders had a special understanding of physical form and spirituality. They clearly wanted the buildings to inspire people to lift their thoughts to the spiritual realm, to appreciate the beauty of creation and majesty of the Divine. It was these cathedral builders, who incidentally kept their knowledge strictly secret, who started Freemasonry.

The mathematicians of antiquity held up geometry as the key to understanding the universe. If we need to pay more attention to geometry, and especially 'sacred' geometry, in order to understand the universe, then perhaps an important function of the crop circles could be to reawaken our interest in geometry?

The English author and publisher John Martineau is fascinated by how sacred geometry is expressed throughout nature. The golden section crops up again and again throughout the natural world, in the very small and the very large relations in the universe. The paths of the planets in our solar system are harmoniously related to each other. The same harmony is visible in every living thing on Earth, from the spiral of a

Indian mandalas

---

8   The vesica piscis is a shape formed by the intersection of two circles with the same radius, in such a way that the centre of each circle lies on the circumference of the other. The name literally means the "bladder of a fish" in Latin (see diagram on page 196 and photo of a double vesica piscis on page 185.

snail's shell to the number of leaves on a twig. There is even a relationship between your own height and the distances between the sole of your foot and your navel and between your navel and the crown of your head. Martineau suggests that sacred geometry, as revealed to us in crop circles, might give us the key to a sort of cosmic DNA (Martineau 1992).

Bert Janssen, a Dutch crop circle researcher who is also very interested in the geometrical aspects of the phenomenon, sees the crop circles as a school for the development of human consciousness. He says that when you enrol in this school and start taking classes, it will change you forever (Janssen 2004).

MUSIC AND SACRED GEOMETRY

Both the Bible and the Koran say that when God created the physical world He began with sound. According to the Indian Rig Veda, the sacred geometrical patterns known as mandalas are expressions of vibrations from the part of the universe which is hidden from human eyes.

Particle physics teaches us that our physical universe doesn't really consist of physical matter. Atoms are composed of neutrons, protons and electrons, which are the same in all matter. These in turn can be divided into elementary particles such as quarks and leptons. But the elementary particles are not material, they consist of energy which is held together by electrical charges. They move in 'orbitals' 'vibrating' at different frequencies which change according to the material's temperature.

Geometry can be defined as numbers expressed in space, while musical scales can be defined as proportions expressed in time. So geometry is closely linked with music. The laws of sacred geometry determine the mathematical intervals which define the western system of musical scales. These intervals are known as diatonic proportions. For example, the interval between the notes G and C is the same as the numerical proportion 3:2.

Sacred geometry is frequently expressed in the patterns and proportions of crop circles. In this way, crop circles are filled with proportions and harmonies which also find expression in the human body, in nature and in the whole of creation.

As early as the 1980s, Dr. Gerald S. Hawkins, the English astronomer who was first to recognise the function of Stonehenge as an astronomical calendar, former professor and chair of the astronomy department at the University of Boston, noticed

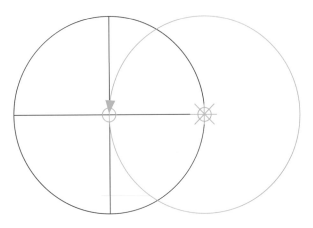

Diagram of vesica piscis

that the components of some crop formations were so placed as to define specific numerical ratios such as 3/2, 5/4 and 9/8. These ratios correspond to the diatonic intervals in western musical scales, in this case to the intervals between a 'fourth', a 'third' and a whole tone (Hawkins 1992).

So we can say that sacred geometry, whether of Gothic cathedrals or crop circles, is a form of 'frozen music'.

Hackpen Hill 1999

THE FIBONACCI SERIES

Mathematician Leonardo Fibonacci lived in Pisa in modern Italy from about 1170 to 1250. He was the man who introduced the Arabic number system to Europe, but he is best known for the number series named after him, the Fibonacci series or golden series, although in fact this was discovered by Indian mathematicians many centuries earlier.

If one begins by adding the numbers 0 and 1 and continues to add each product to the preceding number in the series, one gets the sequence: 0, 1, 1, 2, 3, 5, 8, 13, 21, 34, 55, 89, 144, 233, 377, 610, 987 and so on.

What is so interesting about this series? Well, it turns out that it is the basis for the growth patterns of many natural forms, in both the plant and animal kingdoms.

For example, if we draw a series of rectangles with the lengths of their sides determined by the numbers in the series, and fit a parabolic curve inside the rectangles, we get a perfect representation of how a snail's shell is built up. This curve is known as the Fibonacci spiral or the golden spiral.

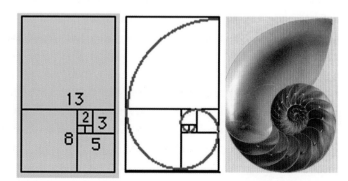

Fibonacci spiral as expressed in a snail shell

Fibonacci spirals in nature

 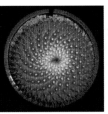  

Many plant parts are built up in accordance with the Fibonacci spiral, for example fir cones, cactuses and the florets of a sunflower. Also, if we take the numbers in the Fibonacci series and divide each by its predecessor, we get the sequence: 5/3 = 1.66..., 8/5 = 1.6, 13/8 = 1.625, 21/13 = 1.61538..., which rapidly approaches the mystical number 1.618034, the ratio of the Golden Mean.

Several crop circles have embodied the Fibonacci series in their designs: the torus knot at Alton Barnes 1997 (photo p. 205); the Julia Set, Stonehenge 1996 (diagram p. 81); the snail shell, Pewsey 2002 (photo p. 178); Hackpen Hill 1999 (diagram p.197); Wayland's Smithy 2006 (photo p. 132).

SOME NOTEWORTHY FORMATIONS
CROOKED SOLEY 2002

On the 28th August 2002, the well known crop circle photographer Steve Alexander heard that a pilot had discovered a striking formation in a wheat field on the Wiltshire / Berkshire border, about 15km east of Marlborough. Alexander decided to fly out to see it straight away, and that proved to be a very smart decision. When he arrived over the site, the farmer had already begun to cut the field. Crooked Soley Farm, where the crop circle was found, is not overlooked by any nearby hills and it's well off the beaten track, so no-one knows how long the formation might have been lying there before it was discovered. As far as we know though, this circle was never visited on the ground before the field was harvested.

Other reasons conspired to draw attention away from Crooked Soley, even after Alexander's aerial photos were published. It was the end of the season for one thing, and only twelve days after the appearance of the 'alien face' formation at Crabwood, which was still capturing the full attention of the whole crop circle world.

However, crop circle enthusiast and geometer Allan Brown set about studying Crooked Soley in detail, worked out how it was constructed and uncovered a whole series of amazing numerological associations hidden in its design. In collaboration with John Michell he went on to publish, in 2005, a 70-page booklet just on this one formation, *Crooked Soley, a Crop Circle Revelation*, which is full of fascinating insights and well worth exploring in full. Here we have space to reproduce only a few highlights of Brown's work (Brown and Michell 2005).

The outline of the formation consisted of a 46 metre diameter central circle of untouched standing crop, surrounded by a 32 metre wide ring of laid crop; within this ring, a pattern resembling a double helix (or a DNA molecule) was composed of hundreds of small 'curved squares' of standing corn.

The central circle was untouched standing crop and the geometrical centre of the whole was several metres from the nearest tramline, so nobody could have stood in the middle to mark out the circle. But this is a minor point. It's the double helix which is interesting.

Allan Brown counted 504 standing clumps of wheat and saw that to draw these curved squares, one would need to create a latticework of 144 arcs throughout the whole ring, defining 792 further squares of laid crop. The thin lines marking out this net can be seen in some places in the photos of the formation. The total number of boxes defined in this way is then 1296 or 6x6x6x6.

Only a section of the arcs used to create the latticework field in figure 1 are used in the actual crop circle, namely those which fall within the 23 m wide band around the central standing circle. But if one takes the whole net, it can be seen as a two-dimensional representation of the three-dimensional figure known in mathematics as a torus, which is basically the same shape as a doughnut.

Having created the latticework field, the makers of Crooked Soley formed the actual pattern by flattening specific curved squares within it. That pattern - a complex and beautiful representation of a twisted DNA double helix structure meeting itself in a ring - is impressive enough in itself, with its perfect six-fold symmetry as well. What makes it even more remarkable is the ratios of the standing and flattened squares.

The numbers 504 and 792, if scaled up by a factor of 10, give some famous numbers which numerologists recognise as having rather unique properties.

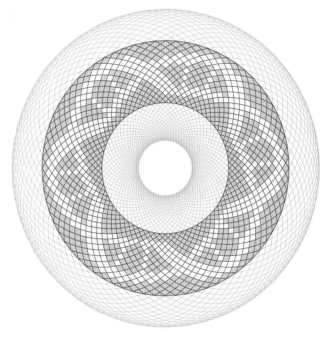

Figure 1: Crooked Soley crop circle with the complete lattice which forms the basis of the pattern (Illustration: Allan Brown)

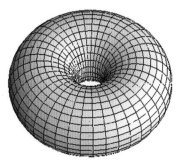

Figure 2: the mathematical figure known as the torus

Facing page: Crooked Soley, August 2002 (Photo: Steve Alexander)

5040 was taken by Plato as the key symbol of the divinely ordered Creation, and he called it 'the heavenly pattern', writes John Michell.

5040 is the product of the first seven numbers, 1 x 2 x 3 x 4 x 5 x 6 x 7, written as 7! or 'factorial 7' in modern maths. But 5040 is also the product of the remaining integers: 7 x 8 x 9 x 10 = 5040! Thus this number is the key to symmetry in the decad of numbers (representing the material world) as they pivot around the mystical number 7, which is the symbol of the universal soul.

Plato believed that for civilised society to be organised in a perfect way, the number of citizens in a community should be 5040 and that this magic number should be the basis for all social structures. Like Plato's Laws, the Revelation of St. John the Divine includes a vision of the heavenly city whose radius was 5040 feet, although it was also said to be square.

In antiquity the circle symbolised Heaven while the square stood for the Earth, the material plane. The mathematical puzzle of 'squaring the circle' symbolises the joining together of the two realms. Squaring the circle involves finding a square which has the same circumference as a given circle and a common centre. The circumference of a circle is given by the formula $2\varpi r$. A good approximation to ϖ is 22/7. If we take a circle with radius 5040 units, its circumference will measure 5040 x 44/7 = 31680. The square which will match that will have a side length of 31680 divided by 4 = 7920.

Figure 3: The numbers 7920 and 5040 express the ratio between the radius and a quarter of the circumference of a circle.
Figure 4: The numbers 7920 and 31 680 (= 44/7 x 5040) express the squared circle
Figure 5: Four circles touching the midpoints of each side of the square have a diameter of 2160
(Illustrations: Allan Brown)

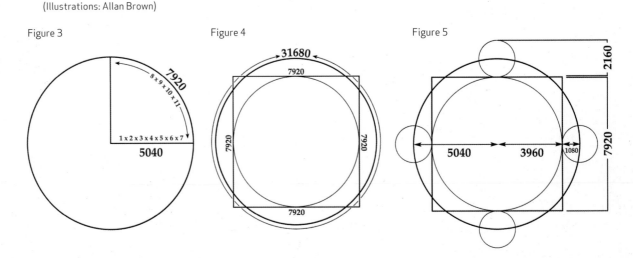

Figure 3   Figure 4   Figure 5

Facing page: Straight Soley July 2006
(Photo: Steve Alexander)

So, the numbers 5040 and 7920 express the squaring of the circle. In the illustration below (?) we see how the maximum distance between the side of the square and the circumference of the circle can be used to find the radius of four small circles placed touching the midpoints of each side of the square. Their diameter will be 2160. Michell goes on to draw parallels with the Great Pyramid at Cheops and to explain how the numbers 504 and 792 recur in the layout of ancient monuments such as the stone circles at Stonehenge. Not only that, even the relative sizes of the Earth and the Moon fit the same numerical patterns, when measured in English miles. So if you place the Moon touching the Earth, the centre of the Moon gives you the radius to draw a circle which can be squared by putting a box around the Earth!

In the booklet mentioned, Brown and Michell find many more examples of numerical correlations related to the numbers implied by the Crooked Soley crop circle and they range far and wide through cosmology, numerology and sacred geometry. However they also return to the subject of crop circles. When Brown looked at the circle squaring diagram he had drawn in Figure 5 (p.200), it looked suspiciously familiar. Then he realised: the number and the relative sizes of the small circles and the large one was the same as he had already seen in numerous other crop circles, namely in the 'quintuplets' which were so common in the 1980s and 1990s. He got out his drawings of these old formations and confirmed his insight. It was as if for 20 years the phenomenon had been trying to show us these relationships, but we just didn't get it, until at last the circle makers were forced to write it out in big letters for us - by making the formation at Crooked Soley (Brown and Michell 2004)!

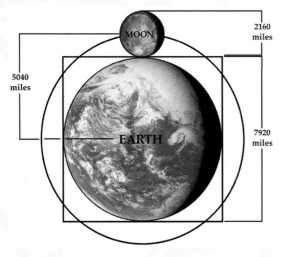

Figure 6: The relative sizes of the Earth and the Moon fit the numbers 5040 and 2160 thus expressing the squared circle
(Illustration: Allan Brown)

STRAIGHT SOLEY 2006

This summer, several Wiltshire crop circles featured patterns of nested crescents which seemed to have a three-dimensional character. For years these kinds of patterns have been used as illustrations of 'time tunnels' and 'wormholes'. Wormholes were first suggested and later popularised by the famous American astrophysicist Carl Sagan. The idea of a wormhole is that if space-time can be strongly 'curved', then a kind of tunnel might be possible as a short-cut across the curvature. This would then allow travel over enormous distances at faster-than-light speeds (read more about

Right: Aldbourne, 2006 (Photo: Axel Kayser)
Top: Windmill Hill, June 2006 (Photo: Steve Alexander)
Above: Savernake, Forest July 2006 (Photo: Axel Kayser)

Facing page, top right: Woodborough Hill, July 1997 (Photo: Lucy Pringle)
Facing page, centre right: Etchilhampton, August 2006
(Photo: Axel Kayser)

travelling through worm-holes in Carl Sagan's science fiction novel Contact.

Why would so many crop circles that summer appear to take up this theme? Did the patterns show that crop circles are a sort of portal for travelling into the past, into the future or to distant places in the universe? Are the crop circles themselves a sort of communication across space and time, or do the patterns seek to point out that time, as we experience it, is an illusion? Could the message be that we are approaching a new era where time as we experience it will no longer exist.

Barely a kilometre east of Crooked Soley Farm lays Straight Soley Farm. On 20th July 2006 an unusual and beautiful crop circle appeared which seemed to me to represent the crowning glory of the 'time tunnel' patterns. I interpret it as two wormholes surrounded by an interference pattern.

The torus is a three-dimensional surface, as mentioned. Several crop circles have shown a torus in a two-dimensional representation. The best known example is the formation at Woodborough Hill which appeared in 11th July 1997.

It's interesting that in mathematical terms it's also possible to imagine a four-dimensional torus. This can be visualised by turning the torus inside out and flattening it out. Read more about torus maths at www.math.brown.edu.

 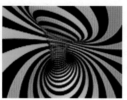 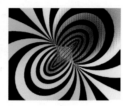

| A torus from the outside | The inside of a torus, partially opened out | The inside of a torus, fully flattened out |

If we do that, we can see that the inside of a torus looks like a wormhole in curved space-time (above)! Therefore the crop circle at Straight Soley shows a representation of a four-dimensional torus! Note also that at the centre of the flattened torus there is a diamond-like pattern of crossing arcs. This diamond figure is not included in the centre of the 20th July crop circle pattern. Instead we see two diamond shapes just above and below the centre. On the 15th August the same year, however, the missing piece of the jigsaw turned up in the shape of a new crop circle at Etchilhampton Hill. That formation included the missing piece in the shape of a diamond of exactly the same shape as the one in the centre of the visualisation of the flattened torus (photo to the right).

BARBURY CASTLE, WILTSHIRE 2008

Midway between Avebury and Swindon where the Ridgeway skirts the edge of the Marlborough Downs, the Iron Age hill-fort of Barbury Castle sits in a prime position on top of Barbury Hill. One of the most prominent hill forts in the area, Barbury offers fine views to the north and west, and overlooks fields which have hosted many crop circles over the years. These include the famous triangular formation from 1991, but also an even more amazing circle which appeared on 1st July 2008.

This formation, discovered by walkers on the Ridgeway, and photographed from

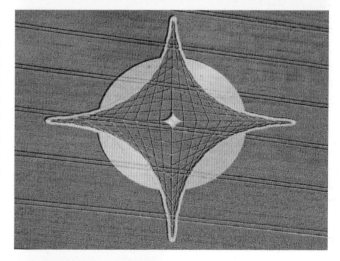

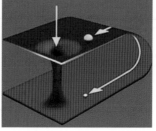

Curved space-time with wormhole

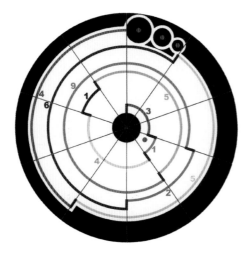

π 3.141592654...

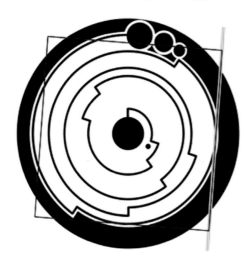

Top: Explanatory diagram, Barbury Castle June 2008 (Illustration: Michael Glickman)
Over: Diagram with bridleway (brown line) squaring the circle (Illustration: Bert Janssen)
Facing page: Barbury Castle June 2008 (Photo: Gary King)

the air the same day, was in a field of barley just north of the hill. Similarities were immediately apparent with the 1991 formation, notably the 'ratchet' appearance of the spiral corridor, which also featured in one of the corners of the earlier formation (photo p. 9). Another noticeable feature was that a bridleway cut right through the formation. It was few days before the pattern was decoded. Retired professor of architecture and prolific crop circle researcher Michael Glickman and retired physicist Mike Reed both worked out the puzzle. First divide the circle up into 10 sectors of 30 degrees each, along the lines of the steps in the ratchet (the thin blue lines in the figure on the left). Starting at the centre, count the number of sectors crossed by each separate arc in the spiral. Note that after the first arc, counting 3 sectors, there is a very small circle in the corn, representing a decimal point, so we have 3.1. The number series continues and many people will soon spot the number π (Pi), which is given to nine decimal places: 3.141592654. The pattern even shows elegantly, with three 'dots' after the last '4', that π is an irrational number which continues indefinitely!

Michael Glickman had not been able to visit any crop circles for several years on account of ill health - until Barbury castle. Thanks to the bridleway he could be pushed in his wheelchair all the way into the formation! It wasn't hard to understand why the circle had been placed just there in that field: so that Glickman would be able to visit it, of course! When I arrived in Wiltshire a few weeks later and met Glickman, he explained to me why he thought this formation was the most important one ever: because it demonstrated π, which is the key to squaring the circle. Squaring the circle symbolises the sacred union between heaven and Earth and it is just this union which the formation represents, says Glickman. Heaven has come down to Earth. The squared circle shows us that heaven and Earth are one and that we humans must begin to relate to the universe as a part of it, rather than as an isolated appendage.

A few weeks later, Bert Janssen discovered another important thing about the Barbury pi-formation. The bridleway which seems to cut through the circle is not accidentally aligned. It forms one side of a square with the same circumference as the outer circle in the formation. In other words, the bridleway squares the circle! (Crop Circles and More).

THE MAYAN CALENDAR

Anyone who has come into contact with New Age media in recent years has no doubt heard of 'the Mayan calendar' and the 'year 2012'. The Mayan Indians of Central America had a simple solar calendar of 365 days like our own, known as the Haab. But they also had a very complex and quite different calendar which was entirely independent of the movements of the heavenly bodies.

This 'sacred calendar', also known as the Tzolkin, was used for religious purposes. The Swedish author of the book "The Mayan Calendar and the Transformation of Consciousness", Carl Johan Calleman, is considered a leading international expert on the Mayan calendars. According to him, the Tzolkin has a spiritual perspective on time and expresses the god-given rhythms of the cosmos and the development of consciousness in the universe. This calendar was based on two different 'week' systems, one numbered and one named. With 13 days in the 'numbers' week and 20 in the 'names' week, it took 260 days to go the whole round and begin again.

To measure longer periods of time, the Maya used a third system called the 'Long Count' made up of 13 'baktuns'. A baktun is again made up of 400 tuns (a tun is a 360 day period), and is the equivalent of 394 ordinary sun years. 13 baktuns thus define a period of 5125 years. Most archaeologists agree that the starting date for the long count was 11th August 3114 BC. 13 baktuns after this date, is 21st December 2012.

The Meso-American peoples shared a concept which Carl Johan Calleman calls "cycles of emergence". Their complex and precise calendar system reflects this understanding of human existence perfectly. One of these cycles is represented by the nine levels of creation called the 'underworlds'. They make up nine levels of consciousness development, and are symbolised in the nine steps of some Mayan pyramids. Each of the nine levels is controlled by a particular energy (expressed as a Mayan god) and builds on the experiences of the previous level. The first level represents a period of several million years, the second several hundred thousand years, the length of each period getting shorter as we move up the levels, the last level lasting only 7 months. We are now on the ninth and last level which began in February 2011 and ends in October 2011 (Calleman 2005).

In recent years there has been great interest in the Mayan calendars, both amongst New Agers and in Hollywood. There has been a tendency in both arenas to present December 2012 as the date prophesied by the Mayans for the end of the world. However there's no indication that the Mayans thought anything of the kind, rather they believed that a new series of cycles and a new age will begin then. If you want to learn more about the Mayan calendar, I highly recommend Carl Johan Calleman's book and his website called the Mayan Calendar Portal (mayaportal.lucita.net/).

Now let's look at some crop circles which have been seen by some crop circle enthusiasts as having a connection with the Mayan calendars.

Wakerley Woods 2001 (Photo: Nick Nicholson)

WAKERLEY WOODS 2001

This crop circle (right) was found on 3rd June 2001, not far from the town of Leicester. The pattern has certain similarities to symbols used in the Mayan calendar. There is an outer ring with 18 symbols, a middle ring with 9, and an inner ring with 18 symbols again. The number 18 is used in the greater baktun system. A baktun is built up like this: 20 days make a uinal, 18 uinal makes a tun (360 days), 20 tuns make a katun and 20 katun make a baktun. The number 9 could refer to the levels of evolution of consciousness mankind is supposed to go through.

WAYLAND'S SMITHY 2005

This spectacular crop circle (see picture p.14) was reported on 9th August from near the Neolithic passage grave at Wayland's Smithy in Oxfordshire. It was associated with the Mayan calendar in this way: the outer ring was made of 20 square boxes. The central area was divided into four sectors each containing 13 lines, making a total of 52 lines. 13, 20 and 52 are fundamental numbers in the Mayan calendar. There are 20 katuns in a baktun and 13 baktuns in the great baktun cycle which ends in 2012. The number 52 is significant because every 52 years, the start of the Haab calendar based on the 365-day solar year and the start of the Tzolkin period of 260-day 'divinatory year' coincide.

PEWSEY 2007

Over the years many crop circles have appeared in the fields under the White Horse of Pewsey. On 4th August 2007 they played host to a circle with Mayan associations. A nine-pointed star was surrounded by a crescent and then a ring divided by 3 small triangular pointers. An outer double ring was divided into 9 sections and finished with 9 larger triangular pointers on the outside circle.

The pattern was seen as a moon and sun calendar pointing to a date 14 days later, the 18th August. Another formation which appeared at Stanton St. Bernard on 13th

Right: Pewsey White Horse, August 2007 (Photo: Axel Kayser)

August also seemed to point to that date, on which Venus was conjunct the Sun (in a straight line with Earth).

On the other hand, another expert on the Mayan calendar, Michelle Jennings, read the Pewsey formation as referring to the nine underworlds. She thinks that the small triangular pointers show that our inner, unconscious or intuitive perceptions are now emerging into our conscious lives. The triangles on the outside ring show the potential of our consciousness for unlimited growth which will break all hitherto known barriers.

AVEBURY MANOR 2008

Early in the morning of 15th July 2008, a new crop circle was discovered in a field just north of the henge at Avebury. It was an exact representation of our solar system: a large central circle for the sun, with nine rings around it for the orbits of the planets,

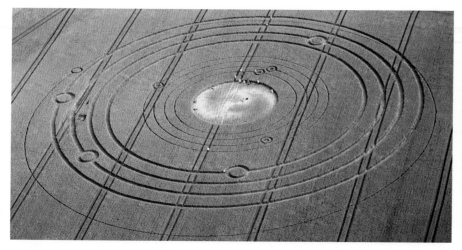

Above: Our solar system with the positions of the planet on 23/12/2012
(Illustration: Nyako Nakar)
Left: Crop circle at Avebury Manor, July 2008 (Photo: Gary King)

and on each ring a smaller ring to represent the planets themselves. The outermost ring, standing for the path of Pluto, was accurately represented as an eccentric orbit crossing inside that of Neptune.

From the middle of the 1990s to the present day there have been several formations showing solar systems. Some people claim to be able to calculate from the positions of the planets in relation to each other what date the snapshot of the solar system might refer to. In this case the result turned out to be 23rd December 2012 (apart from the fact that Pluto was in the wrong place).

The difference between the dates of 23rd December and 21st December (the supposed end date for the Mayan Calendar) can easily be explained. For one thing it depends on when the start date was for the current cycle back in 3,114 B.C. Experts disagree as to whether this would be 11th or 13th August. And with changes to the western calendar both in Roman and Victorian times, as well as inaccuracies over the years, it's not possible to match the dates exactly over such a long time span.

It was frustrating when the farmer (or his employee) damaged the formation the day after it was found. It seems he drove along three of the tramlines with a tractor and a mower and partly flattened the planet Mars, then messed up the central circle by driving backwards and forwards, making the circle into a big rectangle of cut corn and partly obliterating the orbits of Mercury and Venus.

A week later however, on the 22nd July, the formation was repaired and extended!

Above: Formation in barley near Liddington Castle, June 2010
(Photo: Eva-Marie Brekkestø)

The standing corn around the damaged centre rectangle was now flattened so that the central circle got bigger, but Mercury survived as a ring of standing corn in the flattened area. Venus was on the edge of the standing and flattened areas, also still marked with a small ring. Next to the original solar system, a new formation had been made (or at least started?) with a single huge ring and nothing inside. Around this ring however, and dotted around the field, were a number of strange squiggles, spirals and small rings (see photo p213).

Some more or less speculative ideas were voiced about what these additions might mean, including theories about the position of the moon, and comets on a collision course with the Earth. However, the two theories that I was most drawn to were quite different:

(1) the formation had been given an interesting addition so that we shouldn't lose sight of the original crop circle and its meaning and

(2) the formation had been expanded to take up nearly the whole field so that the farmer would understand that he should leave the crop circles and their visitors alone, since if he wanted to destroy the addition as well, he would have to destroy most of the crop in the whole field!

THE DREAM

Those of us who are interested in the crop circle phenomenon are used to hearing the following comment again and again: "There's no mystery about crop circles, they're made by people with ropes and planks". One purpose of this book has been to show that this statement doesn't hold water. I usually respond like this: "If you think that all crop circles are man-made, you're just showing how little you know about the phenomenon".

When we're faced with a mystery, and we discover that we don't get the answers we expect to the questions we ask, we're challenged to re-evaluate our view of the world. At the same time as we go looking for the crop circles in the outside world, we may therefore also embark on an inner journey of exploration.

On these parallel journeys you can get help and guidance from books, websites, films, and not least from the people you'll meet in the crop circles. The most important thing though is that you undertake your own journey and find your own answers. My hope is that this book has contributed in some small way to your journey.

For me, the crop circles represent a page of an alternative and larger reality. The phenomenon gives me a glimpse into an 'unknown room' such as we otherwise only visit in the mysterious world of our dreams. Do you know that dream? You're going round your house and you find there are exciting and mysterious rooms which you've never looked into before.

Was it something like this that the Norwegian poet Olav H. Hauge was talking about in his poem "It's the dream"?

It's the dream we carry
that something wonderful will happen,
that it has to happen –
that time will open,
that the hearts will open,
that the rock face will open,
that springs will gush –
that the dream will open –
that one morning we'll glide
into a harbour we didn't know existed.

By Olav Hauge
Translated by James Green

Above: The repaired and enlarged formation at Avebury Manor, July 2008 (Photo: Eva-Marie Brekkestø)

SOURCES / REFERENCES

CHAPTER 1: WHAT ARE CROP CIRCLES AND WHERE DO THEY OCCUR?

Books, magazines and films

Broadhurst, Paul and Miller, Hamish: *The Sun and the Serpent*, Pendragon Press, Cornwall 1989.

Taylor, Busty and Wheatley, Maria: *Avebury, Sun, Moon and Earth*, Wessex Books 2008.

Websites

Crop circle centre: www.korncirkler.dk

Norwegian crop circle group: www.kornsirkler.no: Relaterte fenomener

Swirled News (2002): www.swirlednews.com/article. asp?artID=396 (Andy Thomas)

CHAPTER 2: THE CROP CIRCLE PHENOMENON FROM A HISTORICAL PERSPECTIVE

Books, magazines and films

Andrews, Colin and Delgado, Pat: *Circular Evidence*, Bloomsbury, London 1989.

Andrews, Colin: Crop Circles, Signs of Contact, New Page Books 2003.

Andrews, William (Ed.): *Bygone Hertfordshire*, Kessinger Publishing, England 2008

Bemister, Margaret: *Thirty Indian Legends of Canada*, Douglas and MacIntyre 1992.

Blyth Gerish, William: *Hertfordshire Folk Lore* (pamphlets 1905–1921), Wakefield 1970.

Brekkestø, Eva-Marie: *Kornsirkler, verdens vakreste mysterium*, Indre ledelse 2004.

Capron, J. Rand: "A short letter to the editor", *Nature* no. 22, 29th July 1880.

Curven, E. Cecil: *Sussex Notes and Queries*, vol.6, 1936–1937.

Delgado, Pat (publisher) *CPR Newsletter* 1984-1992.

Fuller, Paul and Rendall, Peter: *The Crop Watcher*, no. 9, 1989.

Fuller, Paul and Rendall, Peter: *The Crop Watcher*, no. 14, 1992.

Fuller, Paul and Rendall, Peter: *The Crop Watcher*, no. 21, 1993.

Fuller, Paul and Rendall, Peter: *The Crop Watcher*, no. 23, 1994.

Grimm, Jacob and Wilhelm: *Irische Elfenmärchen*, Leipzig 1826.

Heine, Heinrich: *Elementargeister*, Salon Band III 1837.

Hellström, AnneMarie: *En Krönika om Åsbro*, Bokforlaget Libris Örebro, Malmö 1990.

Loosley, William Robert: *An Account of a Meeting with Denizens of Another World 1871*. Edited with a

commentary by David Langford, St. Martin's Press, New York 1979.

Magee, Judith: "Queensland again", *The Australian Annual Flying Saucer Review* (UFOIC Edition), no. 2, 1966.

McCormack, Ian and Anthony Horn: *The Circle Hunter Magazine*, no. 3, 1994.

Meaden, Terence: "Major Developments in Crop Circle Research in 1990: Part 2", *Journal of Meteorology*, U.K., 16:127, 1991 (1).

Meaden, Terence (Ed.): *Circles from the Sky*, Souvenir Press 1991 (2).

Müller, Andreas: *Kornkreise: Geometrie, Phänomene, Forschung*, AT Verlag 2001.

Anderhub, Werner and Müller, Andreas: *Phänomen Kornkreise*, AT Verlag 2005.

Mutwa, Credo: *Isilwane: The Animal. Tales and Fables of Africa*, Cape Town, S. Africa, Struick 1996.

Plot, Robert: *A Natural History of Staffordshire*, Oxford 1677.

Randles, Jenny and Fuller, Paul: *Crop Circles, a Mystery Solved*, Hale London 1990.

Randles, Jenny and Fuller, Paul: *Crop Circles, a Mystery Solved*, 2nd ed., Hale London 1993.

Remigius, Nicolaus: *Daemonolatria – das ist – Von Unholden und Zaubergeistern*, Frankfurt 1590.

Silva, Freddy: *Secrets in the field*, Hampton Roads Publishing Company, Charlotteville, Canada, 2002.

Svahn, Clas: *UFO-mysteriet, från flygande tefat till cirkler i sädesfelten*, Parthenon förlag, Nyköping, Sweden 1998.

Sussex Notes and Queries 1932 – quarterly journal of the Sussex Archaeological Society, nr. 6, 1936–1937. Edited by Mary S. Holgate, F. S. A., Sussex Archaeological Society, Barbican House, Lewes 1937.

Thomas, Andy: *Fields of Mystery*, SB Publications, East Sussex, England 1996.

Thomas, Andy: *Vital Signs*, SB Publications, East Sussex, England 1998.

Wilson, Terry: *The Secret History of Crop Circles*, The Centre for Crop Circle Studies 1998.

Websites

BBC: www.bbc.co.uk/ww2peopleswar/stories/95/a3940995.shtml BBC's online archives 2005. Wales 1941

CPR (Circles Phenomenon Research International): www.colinandrews.net/Crop_Circle_Research.html (Colin Andrews)

Crop Circle Archive: www.cropcircle-archive.com (Berthold Zugelder ed.)

Crop Circle Science: www.cropcirclescience.org

ICCRA: The Independent Crop Circle Researchers Association: www.iccra.org (Jeffrey Wilson ed.)

Swirled News (2005): www.swirlednews.com/article.asp?artID=844 (Andy Thomas)

CHAPTER 3: EYEWITNESS REPORTS

Books, magazines and films

Andrews, Colin and Pat Delgado: *Circular Evidence*, Phanes Press, London 1989.

Brekkestø, Eva-Marie: *Kornsirkler, verdens vakreste mysterium*, Indre Ledelse 2004.

Corliss, William: "Mystery Spirals in Cereal Field", *Science Frontiers* no. 31, 1984.

Fuller, Paul and Rendall, Peter: *The Crop Watcher*, no. 12, 1991.

Fuller, Paul and Rendall, Peter: *The Crop Watcher*, no. 13, 1992.

Fuller, Paul and Rendall, Peter: *The Crop Watcher*, no. 16, 1993.

Gazecki, William: *Crop Circles, Quest for Truth*, documentary film, USA 2002.

Hesemann, Michael: *Crop Circles, The Cosmic Connection*, Gateway, Bath England 1996.

Janssen, Bert and Janet Ossebaard: *Contact with the unknown intelligence behind the crop circles*, documentary film, Netherlands 2001.

Meaden, Terence: "The Circles Effects and its Mysteries", *Journal of Meteorology* 1989.

Meaden, Terence: "Major Developments in Crop Circle Research in 1990: Part 2", *Journal of Meteorology*, U.K., 16:127, 1991 (1).

Meaden, Terence (ed.): *Circles from the Sky*, Souvenir Press, 1991 (2).

Meaden, Terence (ed.): *Journal of Meteorology*, Wiltshire, England.

Michel, Aime: *Flying Saucers and the Straight Line Mystery*, Criterion Books, USA 1958.

Müller, Andreas: *Kornkreise, Geometrie, Phänomene, Forschung*, AT Verlag, München 2001.

Anderhub, Werner and Müller, Andreas: *Phänomen Kornkreise*, AT Verlag, München 2005.

Pix-People Magazine, 1(4), 1972, SA 1968-001 Australia

Randles, Jenny and Paul Fuller: *Crop Circles*, a Mystery Solved, Hale, London 1990.

Randles, Jenny and Paul Fuller: *Crop Circles, a Mystery Solved*, 2nd edition, Hale, London 1993.

Shuttlewood, Arthur: *The Warminster Mystery*, Tandem, London 1976

Svahn, Clas: *UFO-mysteriet, från flygande tefat till cirkler i sädesfälten*, Parthenon förlag, Nyköping 1998.

The Daily Star, 23rd May 1969, Sudbury, Ontario Canada

Thomas, Andy: *Fields of Mystery*, SB Publications, East Sussex 1996.

Thomas, Andy: *Vital Signs*, SB Publications, East Sussex 1998 (new edition 2002).

Trainor, Joseph: "UFOs leave two crop circles in Brazil", *UFO Roundup*, no. 10, vol. 2, 9. Mars 1997.

Wilson, Terry: *The Secret History of Crop Circles*, The Centre for Crop Circle Studies, 1998.

Wingfield, George: "The Crop Circles", *The Cereologist*, no. 2, 1991.

Wingfield, George: "The Evolving Crop Circles", *The UFO Report* 1992, ed. Timothy Good (Sidgwick & Jackson Ltd, London).

Websites

AUFORN (Australian UFO Research Network Archives): www.auforn.com/1975.htm

BLT Research (2001): www.bltresearch.com/eyewitness/eyewitness1.php

BLT Research (2003): www.bltresearch.com/eyewitness/eyewitness5.php

BLT Research (2006): www.bltresearch.com/eyewitness/eyewitness7.php

BLT Research (2008): www.bltresearch.com/eyewitness/eyewitness8.php

British Ministry of Defence: "UFO Sightings across the West in the late Eighties and early Nineties", document declassified 20th October 2008. Referred to on www.thisiswiltshire.co.uk, 21/10/2008.

Crop Circle Connector (2005): www.cropcircleconnector.com/archives/2005/wadenhill/wadenhill2005a.html (Mark Fussell ed.)

Duper, Nikola 2005: X-Cosmos Italia http://www.x-cosmos.it/news/visualizza.php?id=2908

ICCRA (2003): www.iccra.org/reports/wisconsin_mayville_kekoskee_7_4_2003.htm

Kornkreise Forschung: www.kornkreise-forschung.de/text2005review.htm (Andreas Müller ed.)

NUFORS: www.noufors.com/ufo_landings.html

PRUFOS (Police Reporting UFO-Sightings): prufospolicedatabase.co.uk "On Duty Sightings – C, rapport 149": prufospolicedatabase.co.uk/4.html

Millennium Research: www.cropcircleanswers.com/sightings2.htm (Ed Sherwood ed.)

Swirled News (2002): www.swirlednews.com/article.asp?artID=565

UFO Casebook: ufocasebook.com/physicaltracecases.html

UFORUM database, Australian Society for Psychical Research: htt://members.ozemail.com.au/~amilani/ufo.html (Andrew Milani ed.)

UFOs at Close Sight: www.ufologie.net/1954/20ct1954saintsouplet.htm#1357

CHAPTER 4: LIGHT PHENOMENA, UFOS, WHIRLWINDS AND PLASMA

Books, magazines and films

Abrahamson & Dinniss: "Ball lightning caused by oxidation of nanoparticle networks from normal lightning strikes on soil". *Nature* 403, 2000

Aubrey, John: *A Natural History of Wiltshire*, Wiltshire Topographical Society 1847.

Deveraux, Paul: *Places of Power*, Cassell Illustrated 1999.

Dikhtyar, Jerby E: "Fireball ejection from a molten hot spot to air by localized microwaves". *Physical Review Letters* 96, 2006

Hunt, Robert: *Romances of the West of England*, 1881.

Keio University and Burton Inc: "Three Dimensional Images in the Air", published by AIST (www.aits.go.jp) 7th February 2006

Meaden, Terence: *Circles from the Sky*, Souvenir Press, London 1991.

Scott, Sir Walter: *Minstrelsy of the Scottish Border*, Cadell and Davies, UK 1802.

Wist, Arne: *UFO-mysteriet i Hessdalen*, Bladkompaniet, Oslo 1983.

Websites

BLT Research (2004): www.bltresearch.com/eyewitness/eyewitness2.php

BLT Research (2007): www.bltresearch.com/eyewitness/eyewitness5.php

Keio University and Burton Inc: "Three Dimensional Images in the Air", published by AIST www.aits.go.jp ,7th February 2006

Muir, Hazel: "Lightning balls created in the lab", New Scientist, 10th January 2007 www.

newscientist.com/article/mg19325863.500-lightening-balls-created-in-the-lab.html

Project Hessdalen: www.hessdalen.org

UFO Sverige: www.ufo.se/ (Clas Svahn ed.)

CHAPTER 5: THE CROP CIRCLES ON THE GROUND

Books. magazines and films

Müller, Andreas: *Kornkreise, Geometrie, Phänomene, Forschung*, AT Verlag, Tyskland 2001.

Svahn, Clas: *UFO-mysteriet, från flygande tefat till cirkler i sädesfelten*, Parthenon förlag, Nyköping 1998.

Websites

Culture Crop (2): www.culture-crop.com/2006botley.htm (William Betts ed.)

Culture Crop: www.culture-crop.com/2005goldenballhill.htm

The Modern Antiquarian: www.themodernantiquarian.com/site/3967

CHAPTER 6: CROP CIRCLES IN SCEIENCE AND RESEARCH

Books, magazines and films

Andrews, Colin: *Crop Circles, Signs of Contact*, New Page Books 2003.

Haselhoff, Eltjo: *The Deepening Complexity of Crop Circles*, Frog Ltd, Berkeley, California, 2001.

Jenny, Hans: *Kymatik, Wellen und Schwingungen mit ihrer Struktur und Dynamik*, Basilius Presse, Basel, vol 1 1967, vol 2 1974 (www.cymaticsource.com/).

Measures, Mary and Weinberger, Pearl: "The effect of two sound frequencies on the germination and growth of spring and winter wheat", *Canadian Journal of Botany*, 1st September 1968.

Anderhub, Werner and Müller, Andreas: *Phänomen Kornkreise*, AT Verlag, München 2005.

Pringle, Lucy: *Crop Circles, the Greatest Mystery of Modern Times*, Thorsons 1999.

Silva, Freddy: *Secrets in the Fields*, Hampton Roads Publishing Company, Charlotteville, Canada 2002.

Thomas, Andy: *Vital Signs*, S.B. Publications 2002.

Tompkins, Peter and Christopher Bird: *The secret life of plants*, Harper and Row, New York 1973.

Websites

BLT Research (1): www.bltresearch.com/plantab.php

BLT Research (2): www.bltresearch.com/xrd.php, "Clay-Mineral XRD Study"

BLT Research (3): www.bltresearch.com/magnetic php

BLT Research (4): www.bltresearch.com/published. php

BLT Research (5): www.bltresearch.com/otherfacts. php

Sacred Britain Tours: www.sacredbritain.com/ research-underground.html

CHAPTER 7: WHO OR WHAT MAKES THE CROP CIRCLES AND WHY?

Books, magazines and films

Andrews, Colin and Delgado, Pat: *Circular Evidence*, Bloomsbury, London 1989.

Bura, Paul and Andy Thomas: *Quest for Contact: Crop Circles, Psychics and UFOs*, S.B. Publications, England 1997.

Douglas, Karen: *Charley Knoll, an Archetypal Crop Circle Experience*, Temporary Temples Press, Hampshire England 2004.

Guldbrandsen, Erling and Øivind Varkøy: *Musikk og mysterium*, Cappelen 2004.

Howitt, Peter: *Sliding Doors*. Film, Paramount Pictures, USA 1998.

Anderhub, Werner and Müller, Andreas: *Phänomen Kornkreise*. AT Verlag, München 2005.

Shyamalan, M.N.: *Signs*. Film, Touchstone Pictures, USA 2002.

Ramis, Harold: *Ground Hog Day*. Film, Columbia Pictures, USA 1993.

Toftenes, Terje: *Crop Circles, Crossovers from another Dimension*. Documentary film, Toftenes Multivision as., Norway

Silva, Freddy: *Secrets in the Fields*, Hampton Roads Publishing Company, Charlotteville, Canada 2002.

Walsh, Neale Donald: *Conversations with God*, Barnes&Noble, USA 1996.

Websites

Crop Files: www.cropfiles.it Interviews with several crop circle researchers: www.cropfiles.it/special/ The_Interview.html (2007)

Lucy Pringle: www.lucypringle.co.uk/photos/

CHAPTER 8: WHAT DO THE CROP CIRCLES MEAN?

Books, magazines and films

Brown, Alan and John Mitchell: *Crooked Soley, a crop circle revelation*, Roundhill Press, Brighton 2005.

Calleman, Carl Johan: *The Mayan Calendar and the Transformation of Consciousness*, Bear & Company, Vermont USA 2004

Hawkins, Gerald S.: *Crop Circles: Theorems in Wheat Fields*, Science News, 2nd January 1992.

Janssen, Bert: *The Hypnotic Power of Crop Circles*, Frontier Publishing, Nederland 2004.

Martineau, John: *The Sophistication of Agriglyph Geometry*, Wooden Books 1992 (revised in several later editions).

Martineau, John: *A Little Book of Coincidence*, Wooden Books 1992.

Sagan, Carl: *Contact*, Simon and Schuster Inc. 1985.

Websites

Crop Circle Connector: www.cropcircleconnector.com

Crop Circles and More: www.cropcirclesandmore. com/thoughts/200803snt.html (Bert Janssen)

The Mayan Calendar Portal: http//mayaportal.lucita.net

Facing page: Crop circle below Milk Hill, Alton Barnes July 2010 (Photo: Eva-Marie Brekkestø)

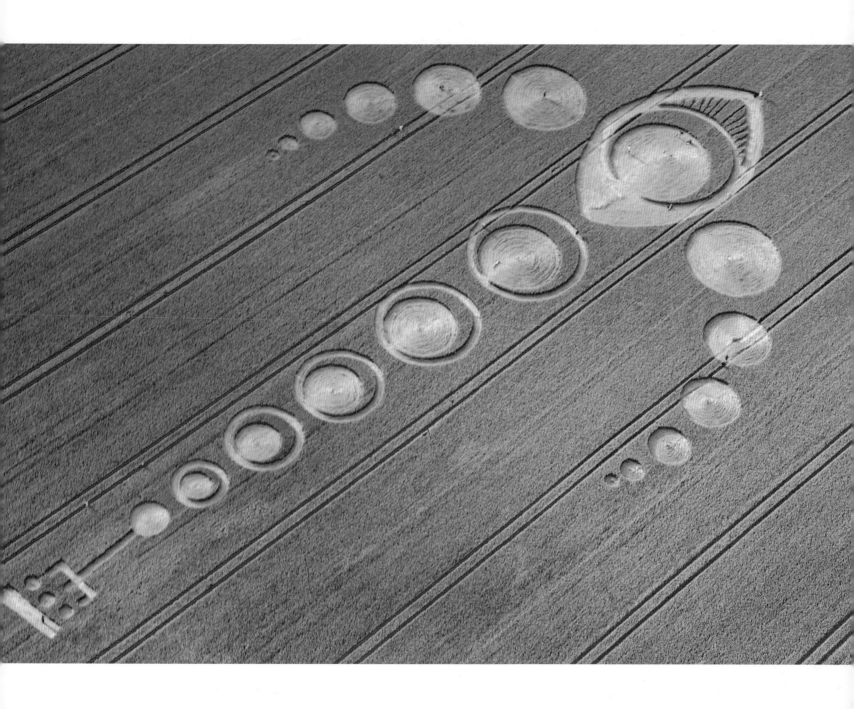